JONAH

Spirituality
of a Runaway Prophet

JONAH

Spirituality
of a Runaway Prophet

Roman Ginn, o.c.s.o.

LIVING FLAME PRESS
LOCUST VALLEY, N.Y. 11560

Scripture quotations are from *The New American Bible.*

Cover: Robert Manning

Nihil Obstat: Rev. George A. Denzer, S.T.D., Censor Librorum, July 29, 1977.

Imprimatur: Most Rev. John R. McGann, D.D., Bishop of Rockville Centre, August 1, 1977.

Published by: Living Flame Press / Locust Valley / New York 11560

Copyright 1978: Gethsemani Abbey

ISBN: 0-914544-21-7

Printed in the United States of America

Dedication

This work is dedicated to the very human author of the book of Jonah who, sometime during the Persian period of world domination (538-331), went through all the thankless toil which writing a book demanded in those primitive days in order to suggest to his fellow countrymen that, since God loves even Israel's ancient enemies, the Assyrians, he must love everybody and consequently so should they.

Contents

Introduction

The book of Jonah is so small that it might be supposed that there is not enough to it to merit a book of meditations. Yet, in spite of its brevity, it contains some of the loftiest spiritual doctrine in the Old Testament. In fact, its fine combination of conciseness and sublimity is what makes it such an ideal subject for spiritual reflection. The Song of Songs is not much longer than Jonah, and yet it was a favorite meditation book for some of the greatest theologians and mystics in the Church. St. John of the Cross, for example, liked it so well that he had it read to him on his deathbed. However, with the more historical-literal approach to the Bible that prevails today, the Song of Songs no longer exercises the same appeal. We feel much more attracted to a book like Jonah in which we can focus our modern problems. Were St. Bernard here today, it is quite possible that instead of over eighty sermons on the Song of Songs, he would give us an equal number on Jonah. Although it is commonly accepted that the book is fiction, it speaks to us from the very real historical situation of its author where it answered some of the problems which troubled the people to whom it was

9

originally addressed. The conviction that it can help us today with our modern post-Vatican II difficulties has motivated these brief reflections.

Since this is not a commentary on Jonah but rather a series of reflections, our approach is circular as well as linear, the meditations being grouped according to themes which follow the chronological sequence of the story.

God Calls Man

This is the word of the Lord that came to Jonah, son of Amittai: "Set out for the great city of Nineveh, and preach against it." *(Jonah 1:1-2)*

The book of Jonah opens with a vocation and an act of disobedience. Together they symbolize the whole of salvation history, which is basically God's quest for rebellious man. The Bible is the record of God's successive interventions into human history to catch up with fleeing man. Biblical history does not open in Eden, with philosophical speculations, but with Abraham's call and his obedience to that call. For unlike Jonah, when Abraham was asked to leave his home and set out on a mission to the unknown, he obeyed and left the program in God's hands. We find in him the model believer in whom faith's structure is evident: renunciation of the security of one's own home, which one has conquered and cultivated, in order to live in faith and fidelity in the land to which God calls. But along with the past, Abraham also had to renounce the future by leaving himself open to God's direction. Even the faith of Jesus, himself, will have this same

11

structure. He will follow his Father's will, in faith, by accepting the humble form of messianic mission chosen for him by his Father instead of the glorious and violent one suggested by some of his followers.

Just how God's word came to Jonah is not clear. The story opens with, the simple majesty of the great prophetic vocations, such as those of Jeremiah and Isaiah. The content of the word, however, is very clear: leave all, go to Nineveh and preach against it. To understand what this meant for Jonah we have to remember that Nineveh, situated on the east bank of the Tigris, was number one among the cities of its day. Although the glory of "the great city" was only going to last for about a century, yet that glory was God's work and, as the end of the book brings out, has its part to play in the story. We must remember too that Assyria was famous for its cruelty. Some texts preserved from its ruins leave no doubt about this. Mass deportations, impalement and blinding of prisoners, etc., were common tasks assigned to Assyrian soldiers. No wonder Jonah balked!

We all want to be sanctified in ideal conditions. We can't understand why God should choose to put us in a position which to our way of thinking is just what we don't need to bring us to Christian maturity. But this is one of the constants in God's way of acting toward us which the Bible reveals. He doesn't put those he loves in ideal conditions. Look at the spot he chose for his own people. If he wanted them to develop free from idolatry, why didn't he pick a more isolated place for them to live in? Palestine was the hot corner of the ancient Near East. The great powers envied it because of its access to the sea and its key position on the road between Egypt and Mesopotamia, as well as between the latter and the western world. What a place to pick! But God chose it because it was not ideal. He wanted the Israelites to live in a country that would keep them spiritually alert. He wanted them to be forced constantly to choose between himself and idols. He didn't want their election to become a pillow to sleep on, but a stimulus to faith and fidelity. This is his reason for sending a vacillating and self-willed, blood and thunder prophet like Jonah to preach in Nineveh.

In Jonah's call we find the structure of every Christian vocation: leave all — home and family — and go to the task God designates with its further development hidden and with no assurance about just how it will turn out. God makes no promise of success. Jonah must go in faith. He must drop his own plans and be incorporated into those of God. What about his family, his harvest, his country? All these are left when God's imperative will descends into his life offering him a program not entirely to his taste.

Anyone who has tried to live in a permanent attitude of openness to the Holy Spirit will not judge Jonah harshly. It is an heroic task. Yet it is the only attitude that does justice to the Spirit's function in the Church. For if the Christian is called to be another Christ, his relation with Christ must be more than that of a disciple to his departed master. There must be some power within the Church, and within the heart of every Christian, that guides and aids this tremendous work of transformation into Christ. This power is the Holy Spirit. He makes Christ present to us and directs our efforts at walking in his footsteps. We are not left with only a book in which to look up what we are to do next, how we are to believe and behave. The Spirit is within us to breathe life into the Bible, to indicate which of its teachings we need at the present moment and to interpret its meaning.

So our programs must always contain a blank space to be filled in by the Spirit when and how he sees fit.

We must remember that behind Jonah lies the long history of Israel's humiliation at the hands of the great powers. Assyria had wiped out Israel, the northern kingdom, and Babylonia carried Judea into a long captivity from which it emerged to become a colony or vassal state under the Persians, Greeks and Romans. It tasted only one brief period of independence under the Maccabees. Hence, there was intense national feeling and strong hatred of foreigners in the Jewish heart. Israel had good reasons for its prejudices and narrowness, as we often have for ours. And we can understand how God's call was diametrically opposed to Jonah's own feelings.

Whoever the author of Jonah was, he believed that God had manifested himself in history and wanted to understand the meaning of that manifestation. He realized that the words God addressed to his people through the prophets and sacred writers, and the faith they had awakened in man, touched upon and actualized a capacity located in the deepest center of man's being: his need to remember, know and love God, which makes him God's image. And since faith is a foretaste of the future vision of God, it releases a necessity to anticipate its contents, even though this anticipation is only partial. This is what stirred him to theological reflection. He wanted to know more about the nature of his God and about his action in history and, at the same time, prepare himself and others for fuller meetings with God in the future, thus helping them and himself to realize their vocations as images of God.

In whatever way Jonah's call came to him, he perceived it as something real. He manifested no fear of being deluded by a false call and showed no anxiety about being tempted to lead an unreal existence by following it. Partly because of the influence of Freud and Marx, modern man is unusually sensitive to any accusation of unreality in his life and desires above all to root his existence in what is real. Hence the Christian vocation must be presented today as emerging from reality, from its very source, and as illuminating the real and directing man toward it. Rather than denaturalizing or distorting what is real, as he is frequently accused of doing, the Christian is called to explain the meaning of the whole of reality and to show man more of its possibilities and dimensions than he could find by himself. For unlike many of his contemporaries, who prefer to be content with the little scraps of reality that their senses offer them rather than have the courage to believe in something infinitely more wonderful but unverifiable by ordinary means, the Christian dares to affirm the existence of an entirely new zone of reality revealed by Christ which gives new meaning to everything else.

Believing as he did in the reality of his vocation, and in the reality of the source from which it sprang, Jonah felt no burning need to prove to others the practical efficacy of his faith. He was living in a period of history when the relation of religion to life was taken for granted. Everyone considered his relation to his gods as something that affected his daily existence very acutely. If the gods were angry, calamities would befall man. If the gods were content, man would enjoy a happy and prosperous life. But today in the face of so many accusations that Christianity has lost its capacity to meet the needs of our time, to clarify them and to deal with them creatively, the convinced Christian may be tempted to think that his primary duty is to prove to others that his faith is not a path to sweet unreality, but to a fuller and more efficacious confrontation with the historical and concrete everyday problems of man — but this is simply not true. The Christian's primary testimony is to the reality of God, before whom he exists in absolute gratuity and filial love. This adhesion to God in pure faith and love is not given as a means of producing any practical effects in the everyday world, but is man's only adequate response to God. The Christian meets God in Christ and loves him because he is who he is: God. This encounter with God will and must necessarily create a real urgency for a concrete love and service of men, but it can never be subordinated to it.

One of the most pleasing features about the little book of Jonah is that its message is presented so gently. It doesn't threaten the reader with deportation, destruction and disaster as the books of the historical prophets do. It puts its message in the form of humorous satire, which makes its point as caustically, but without breaking down the psychological defenses men spontaneously erect when they are faced with aggressiveness and scalded with insults by the Lord's preachers. For our author realized that humor is an expression of man's perennial capacity to transcend even the most apparently impossible situations. Humor is also part of the Christian vocation as an expression of the joy and liberty which flow from the resurrection. In the post-Vatican II Church, humor will help us more in solving our problems than a false sense of the tragic or a passion for polarization.

Even though Jonah didn't go the right way, at least he obeyed the first part of God's command which in Hebrew reads: "QUM." "Get up!" Jonah "qumed" all right, but went the wrong way. One of the problems in modern society is the large number of people whose existence is really no problem for them. They are hardly aware of conditions around them. They live submerged in their daily routine without any ambition to do anything better than what everybody else does: eat and drink, marry and procreate, work and rest. This type of existence, which the existentialists term "inauthentic," is found at all social levels and in all regions of the world. It implies a refusal of man's vocation to become authentically human by rising above the material, social-economic conditions of his life. Rather than take the road to Joppa, these people take no road at all. They don't even heed the first part of God's command. Nothing but a great shock or tragedy, or a very clear perception of life's meaning will be able to stir them into reflection.

Jonah did the first thing necessary for authentic existence: he got up. But it is also necessary to head in the right direction. It is not enough to begin living for an ideal, we must also live for the right one. We don't all have Jonah's privilege of a direct word from God pointing out the right direction. Most of us have to try several roads, head out in several directions successively in pursuit of several ideals before we finally find the right one. But if we remain open to God, if we listen to his voice speaking in our hearts, we will gradually rectify our choice and at last take the road to Nineveh even if, like Jonah, we have to be purified in a whale's belly first. By searching for an ideal, for authentic existence, we are better off than those who sit in the shadow of inauthenticity all their lives with no desire to do better.

Jonah is a symbol of the meaning of human existence. Meaning is used here in the sense of direction. Is life going anywhere, has it a direction to someone or something, or is it just an aimless wandering in a trackless desert? Jonah shows us that God has put meaning in human life. He calls every man to not only get up and live for something, but to head in some precise direction, to live for some concrete ideal. He sends man on a mission. He gives him a vocation. This vocation is twofold: eternal and temporal. Every man has an eternal vocation to become a child of God and to live forever with God after death. His temporal vocation will be the means by which he attains this eternal vocation. God will assign him a specific task to do in this world. To refuse this task means taking the road to Tarshish, choosing to wander after a false vocation instead of assuming the one God indicates. It means heading for a new form of inauthenticity. If our self-chosen, false ideal has some real value, it may lead us back to the road to Nineveh. But this will only occur after passing through the whale's belly and losing lots of time in the process.

Jonah makes it clear that the deciding factor in the success or failure of every man's life is his own free will. He can choose his road. He can go where God wants him to go and so make his life a howling success, or he can freely choose failure. There was no pressure on Jonah to go to Joppa. The text gives no reason for thinking that social or economic causes motivated his decision. The Bible presents man as created to be God's image or representative in the world. His decisions are located in his heart. "With closest custody, guard your heart, for in it are the sources of life." (*Proverbs 4:23*)

What are the means by which God calls the modern Jonah to some particular function in today's Church? He cannot be expected to send an angel as he did to Gideon. Nor can the Christian be expected to feel an irresistible urge to set out for Nineveh, for God's call is not anterior but rather

18

interior to man's liberty, i.e. he always gives him, together with the call, the capacity to accept or reject it. Jonah makes that clear. However an interior urge to take on some function or other can be a real call from God, provided there is nothing in the person's life which makes it obvious to the community that he is lacking in some of the qualities demanded by the New Testament for that particular vocation. But more often God calls Christians through a psychological or religious attraction for a function. One feels drawn to the priesthood or religious life. This attraction must be checked by a psychological examination to be sure that what moves us on the surface of our minds really squares with the motives operating deep within. The ancient Church contains many examples of men called to an office through direct petition by the community. They often had no attraction or urge to take the job, but were pushed by their fellow Christians. Some of the greatest bishops in the Church — St. John Chrysostom, St. Augustine, St. Ambrose, for example — all found their way into their office by this means. It is certainly a safer sign of God's call than the psychological one. Another form in which the vocation may come is through a Christian's simple awareness that he is needed in a particular spot. The call reaches him through the mute voice of the situation. Aside from all the different forms God's invitation may be clothed in, the Christian's own feelings on the subject must always be verified and approved by and in the community.

Good theologian that he was, the author of Jonah was trying to make their faith more intelligible to his contemporary coreligionists. There were many unfulfilled prophecies against foreign nations recorded in the sacred books. Ezekiel had foretold Tyre's destruction *(chapter 26)*. It never came. Obadiah promised the same for Edom. Nothing happened. Isaiah 13 said that Babylon would be crushed, yet there was enough of it still there in Alexander the Great's time for him to plan to make it his capital. This was a scandal to the Jews. By presenting them a real prophet with a divine message that remained unfulfilled, the author of Jonah relieved many a crisis of faith. He had the realism to face up to the situation, and to try to find out just what God was doing by raising up prophets who apparently foretold things that never came to pass. His short book, which helped his contemporaries understand their vocation better, can assist Christians today in the same way, for many feel that the Church has let them down, that God has let them down. In other words, they feel like poor Jonah when the worm got his gourd.

Man Flees From God

But Jonah made ready to flee to Tarshish away from the Lord. He went down to Joppa, found a ship going to Tarshish, paid the fare, and went aboard to journey with them to Tarshish, away from the Lord. (*Jonah 1:3*)

Especially since World War II, Jonah has become a symbol of the meaning of human existence for many men. He shows us how impossible it is for man to escape God, for he is created according to God's image and retains his incessant desire for his exemplar even in open rebellion against him. If man is a mystery, it is because he is the image of an infinitely mysterious God. If he forgets God's name, he will forget his own too, since it is embedded in that of God. In trying to flee from God, he is really running away from himself for the road to himself will have to pass through God. "Where can I go from your spirit? From your presence where can I flee?" *(Psalm 139:7)*

Jonah is a symbol of something in every Christian that resists God's will. He is a hero of human resistance to God's plans in the world and therefore the hero of a lost cause.

One motive for Jonah's flight to Tarshish was fear of failure. He wanted so much to be a successful prophet, a real achiever. When he promised his audience fire and brimstone, he wanted it to happen. Otherwise he would find his reputation ruined and his work exposed to ridicule. But he knew that in dealing with God he couldn't count on sure destruction after he had foretold it, because God had a way of slipping in hanging clauses which conditioned the prophecy. This trick was referred to in prophetic circles as the "conversion condition." It meant that if the people did penance, the destruction was called off. But then how would people know if the disaster would really have taken place if they had done no penance? In other words, there would always be a cloud of uncertainty hanging over him. Some were sure to sneer that he was just a phony. He predicted destruction and none followed. He couldn't bear the thought. Better head for Tarshish until the whole thing blew over. God would find another prophet for that nasty job and, when something came along more to Jonah's liking, he would accept the call. We could be sure of that!

Another motive was sheer fear of the risk involved. What if the Ninevites didn't care for his particular prophetic style at that season of the year? As an Israelite, he was already a stranger in their land. By making a public spectacle of himself as a prophet, he was leaving himself wide open to anything from jeers and insults to stones from the street bouncing off his head. No prudent man would take a risk like that. But Jonah had not only forgotten God's ever-present protection, but also a fundamental law in all human existence: human life is clothed in risk. No man realizes his vocation in clear daylight. There is always uncertainty and obscurity in what he does. Jonah might have remembered too that even staying at home didn't mean security. Many incidents in Israel's history prove this. The priest Micah, for example, was at home when six hundred men from Dan called on him and kidnapped him (*Judges 18:19f*). And in 1 Kings 13 we find a prophet walking home after his message had been delivered when a lion met and killed him. No one can live without risk, and the more authentically one tries to live, the greater will be the danger. Hence risk must be presumed in man's search for authentic existence and especially in performing any mission for God. Jonah's flight from the dangers of Nineveh only led him to more of the same on the sea.

Jonah saw God's will as poison. It would kill him to go to Nineveh. Jesus saw his Father's will as bread; it was his life's source and support. Jonah did not realize that God's will is the source of his own freedom and that by saying no to that will, he shut off the source he was living from. For true freedom is not *from* something, but *for* something. It is the possibility of accomplishing something for God. This is why Jesus was completely free in his obedience to his Father, while Jonah was a slave to the domination of his lower nature and instincts by refusing to obey God. By carrying out his Father's will, Jesus found the strength to perform the greatest task in human history. By wearing himself out in obedience to God's will, Jesus finds his own fulfillment. Jonah's flight only led to misery for himself and others.

We can be grateful today that the biblical concept of liberty, as a possibility for solidarity and service in a community, is replacing the philosophical and individualistic view of freedom as independence and superiority which prevailed during the enlightenment period. Liberty in the Bible is the result of man's relationship with God and incites him to a new relationship with his fellowman. It is a gift rather than a possession, a possibility granted by grace rather than an element of nature. Jonah would have felt very much at home in certain eighteenth century philosophical circles as well as in many modern gatherings. He was doing his thing on his trip to Tarshish; he was doing it his own way. But in the whale's belly he may have learned that he was only really free when he lived in dependence on and abandonment to the one who gave him his liberty.

One of the strongest temptations facing Christians today is the flight from bearing witness to Christ. Some could even be fleeing this responsibility by moving into the anonymity of secular life. For without denying the many good reasons there are for undertaking secular professions and labor, isn't it also possible that there could be some flight from witness involved, some refusal to let our witness to Christ be the whole reason for our existence? Priests and religious, in particular, must ask themselves if they are not fleeing to Tarshish. They must never allow their new involvement in the world to dim their witness to Christ.

Jonah was called to be a witness to the true God in the midst of an idolatrous civilization. His task was to call the most powerful people of his day away from a life of gross materialism and sin to conversion. This meant being a witness to the invisible. This is very hard today. If the Christian could enter the markets of this modern world with a product or service which yielded instant results, he would find open ears. But to talk about an invisible God to men whose noses are moving along the ground in search of more material goods is a thankless task indeed. No wonder Jonah ran away. To be a Christian today means bearing witness to values which can't be verified with the same measures

24

which are valid in other fields.

Jonah is the symbol of a man who resists or flees his vocation because he doesn't like some part of it. He certainly would have liked to go to Nineveh and preach if he could then have sat in his hut and watched the fireworks. But God didn't want any fireworks. Jonah was afraid of this, and so without some guarantee he would not go. He could only accept the mission under condition that the destruction came. He may have mused that he would gladly have borne witness to a God of power and destruction, but he didn't care to work under a God of mercy and forgiveness. The latter was just not his line. He was a power prophet. He had specialized in liquidation jobs. Leave the mercy work to somebody else. He knew his limits and didn't want to go beyond them. A mercy job for a mercy man was his way of thinking. For his part, the more violence the better. Mass destruction was his strong point and it was no time to change. He believed in complementary vocations: blood and gore for him, milk and honey for some other prophet.

Jonah's resistance was really useless. God got what he wanted and Jonah's flight only served God's purpose. The sailors praised God and offered him sacrifices because of Jonah's presence. And the prophet did go to Nineveh and his preaching had just the effect God wanted: conversion. All things work together for the good of those whom God loves, as St. Paul has said *(Romans 8:28)*. In this case the Assyrians are the object of that love. God had the last word. In his love for all men he shuts out any form of particularism: social, ethnic, or religious. He wants all men to be saved and will block our efforts to exclude those we don't like.

Jonah is not merely a literary character but also a symbol of a spirit which prevailed in a large sector of God's people. And Nineveh is not only the capital of Assyria, but a figure of all the foreign capitals of the world: Moscow, Hanoi, Habana, etc.

In our own lives we have to realize that God's will is going to be accomplished in us; his glory is going to shine in us either with or without our consent. He created us for his glory and will not let us slip through his hands. We can run, like Jonah, and find a boat to sleep in, but he will be glorified in our flight and will wake us from our sleep. Hence it is better to cooperate with him willingly in the building up of his kingdom. Each of us is faced with the frightening responsibility of remaining open to his call and of living with the freedom of the autumn leaves, ready to be blown in whatever direction the Spirit may indicate and with no foreknowledge of just what awaits us in the spot where we may be set down. We cannot attach conditions to our response to God. We must answer with the unconditional readiness of the great prophets: "Behold Lord, here I am."

Jonah's great question was: Why pick on me? Why not let some other better qualified prophet go to Nineveh? This is really one of the oldest queries in the Bible. Moses didn't feel he was quite the man for his job. Jeremiah pleaded underage. We can all find reasons for not going to our respective Ninevehs, but God won't be moved. When he has chosen someone for a task, he is closed to all manipulation. Jonah knew this, so he set out for Tarshish.

One of St. Paul's key words is "boasting." It refers to man's tendency to install and insure himself in the world, to set up a dominion which will free him from the future and ultimately from God. Man attempts to extricate himself from his original condition, and to substitute himself for his original cause (God) by means of his adoration of the elements of the world, which Paul names law, flesh, election and promises. Not being able to endure his nakedness before God, man tries to cover himself with anything he can find and then pretends that he is the work of his own hands. He can't bear being constantly reminded of his origin in God's liberty and being exposed to ever new calls from that direction. He can't stand to have God taking care of him, anticipating him and never despairing of him even when he runs away from him and denies him. He doesn't want God to be the way he is. He doesn't want him to be God. So he tries to free himself from God by fulfilling precepts that will cut God down to his size, that will put God on a negotiable level. St. Paul learned this from his own experience. If Jonah had written some letters home while he was under his gourd, we might have had an earlier record of pretty much the same experience.

Nineveh is something different for each of us. For one it may be a home he must stay with, a family he or she has founded and is tempted to desert, an aged person to be cared for. For another it may be a job or some conditions about that job. In every case, Nineveh stands for the disagreeable in our life. Only by keeping the closing scene of Jonah in mind will we understand why God chose us for a particular job and not someone else: because he loves us and wants to teach us to love.

Jonah's problem is not so much disobedience, since he does go to Nineveh after all. His difficulty lies much deeper, as can be seen at the end of the book. He has a real intellectual problem. He just doesn't agree with God's views on the world. God's thoughts are not Jonah's.

One of the most important things we can learn from Jonah today is to live in openness to the Holy Spirit's guidance. For Christianity is not a religion of the book consisting of a mere understanding of doctrine and exemplification of it. It is not centered on the past, even though it is grounded in the past. Its center is the living Spirit of Jesus present within it and directing it at every moment. Hence we cannot live as Christians unless we live in openness to that Spirit. And since the Spirit will very often speak to us through our fellow Christians, we must remain open to their suggestions and views. This means too that we must never feel that we have reached the final stage in our thinking and living, in our theology and spirituality. The truth may still become more evident to us in ways we do not now suspect, and we can only hope to perceive that truth if we maintain a listening and learning attitude. We also have to be ready to be called to new tasks and to explore new horizons. This is one reason why Jonah thought it best to embark for Tarshish.

Certainly one of the most frightening aspects in the call to Nineveh was the solitude it might involve. For the Israelites, solitude was never a source of joy. It was seen rather as an evil, a source of misery and sadness. It also implied additional danger to one's life because of the lack of strength which comes from union with others. The solitary person is regarded as a piece separated from the whole and thus much more vulnerable. Psalm 102 gives an excellent picture of man in solitude:

I am like a desert owl;
  I have become like an owl
    among the ruins.
I am sleepless, and I moan;
  I am like a sparrow alone on
    the housetop. (Psalm 102:7-8)

Lamentations 3:28 uses the same expression to refer to the solitary man as Leviticus 13:46 had employed for the leper: "Let him sit alone and in silence." No wonder Jonah feared this solitude of abandonment, this experience of finding himself used by God for some purpose he didn't understand and which would leave him separated from other men and even from his own aspirations and longings. The Greeks understood the spiritual value of solitude better than the Hebrews. They knew that this experience is often a real necessity for true heroism. Sophocles says that one of his heroes "carries his heart to pasture in solitude." And Oedipus is represented entering into a solitude which is a divine privilege rather than a painful abandonment. He passes through the intense misery of the latter form of solitude to enter another sacred type. He dies alone surrounded by sacred mystery. Thus solitude is both a condemnation and a privilege for him. By embracing the task imposed on him by the gods, the Greek hero is guided by the gods themselves.

It has been said that man fears nothing as much as solitude. Even the thought of death is easier for him to bear than that of complete isolation. Yet this solitude was often demanded by God from some of the most heroic individuals in salvation history. Jeremiah, for example, had to taste it and expressed his reaction in passionate language:

I did not sit celebrating in the circle of merry-
makers;
Under the weight of your hand I sat alone
because you filled me with indignation. (Jere-
miah 15:17)

Ezekiel too had to endure great solitude and abandonment in his mission. But although solitude always meant anguish for the Hebrews, they learned that God could be present even there:

It is good to hope in silence
for the saving help of the Lord.
It is good for a man to bear
the yoke from his youth.
Let him sit alone and in silence,
when it is laid upon him. (Lamentations
3:26-28)

Jeremiah found that his solitude had really brought him closer to God:

Thus the Lord answered me:
If you repent, so that I can restore you,
in my presence you shall stand;
If you bring forth the precious
without the vile,
you shall be my mouthpiece. (Jeremiah
15:19)

It is very probable that poor Jonah was closer to God in the whale than ever before.

Solitude in some form is really an essential part of every Christian vocation, for no one can follow Christ without practicing some sort of separation from other men. This was also true in the Old Testament for the first people of God. Thus God asked Abraham to accept a triple separation:

Go forth from the land of your kinsfolk
and from your father's house to a land that I
will show you. (Genesis 12:1)

This separation will be blessed by the gift of land and posterity. Jacob too found himself "left alone" *(Genesis 32:25)* and obliged to fight an angel all night who left him wounded but blessed. So Jonah's separation from his land and people was nothing unusual. Every great leader among the

Israelites had his share of solitude. Moses was prepared for his call in the desert and, before the great revelation on Sinai, he was separated from those who had ascended the mountain with him *(Exodus 24:2)*. Every Christian, then, must be ready to set out and keep going along the road to Nineveh no matter how much isolation fidelity to his mission will demand. As Jeremiah, the Christian may be thrown out of more than one circle of merry-makers and, like Jonah, he may end up sitting alone under a gourd.

Jonah was cited by St. John of the Cross to illustrate how God's words can be absolute in their form and yet contain some concealed condition, which when fulfilled, leads to the divine words' lack of completion. God's words are always true, but we do not always see the hidden clause upon which their fulfillment depends. The promised destruction of Nineveh did not take place because the cause for the destruction had ceased, i.e. the Ninevites' sins. St. John attributes Jonah's flight to his insight into this mystery. He knew God could slip hidden clauses into prophetic messages and, when he sat in his hut outside Nineveh, he was wondering if there had been one in his. When his fear became a reality, he broke down and wished that he were dead. *(Ascent 2:20)*

We don't know anything about Jonah's past. He may have had previous missions from the Lord on which he proved his worth as a prophet. The rabbis think he won fame as a prophet during the reign of Jeroboam II *(2 Kings 14)*, and was later sent to foretell the destruction of Jerusalem. But the city repented and was spared and this ruined Jonah's reputation. Thus the call to Nineveh came at a time when he was just a little weary of the whole job anyway. He had worked enough and done what he was told. Let somebody else take the job for a change. He may have told himself that if the call had come ten years earlier, he would have gladly accepted. But now, in his mid-forties or fifties . . . perhaps retirement was on his mind when he took ship for Tarshish. The scholars give Spain or Sardinia as the probable location of this region or city. And where could one find a better spot for retirement than Spain or Sardinia? So the trip to Nineveh may be presented to us late in life. We may have settled down to a peaceful existence and may see no great attraction in moving to a metropolis full of dust and noise like Nineveh. But "This is the word of the Lord that came to Jonah. . . . "

Jonah did not want to preach such a human God, a God who came so close to man, a God who was concerned for not only the Assyrians but even for their cattle. He felt that this was no way for God to act. God was almighty and transcendent, infinitely holy and everlasting, but he couldn't be so human. He couldn't lower himself like this. Jonah's criticism is similar to that of the Pharisees in regard to Jesus. Jesus mixed with publicans and sinners. God was doing the same by concerning himself with the fate of those whom the Jews regarded as the earth's scum. The Greek philosopher Celsus would say later that Jesus acted just like someone who was trying to form a band of robbers. He invited the worst elements in society to join him. He looked around for the ignorant, for prostitutes, for collaborators with Rome, etc. Jonah had the same problem with God.

Jonah's message to Nineveh was "different." This was another painful point about the mission. In the Semitic mentality of the time, the individual lived submerged in the collectivity and it required real heroism to walk out of step. Today there is a new form of collective mentality being formed by the mass communication media, which is directed toward the leveling of all men to a standard type. No one today wants to be a permanent voice of discord in humanity's choir. But this is just what the Christian must be prepared to become if he is going to speak the message God gives him to bring to Nineveh. Isaiah found this out:

> For thus said the Lord to me, taking hold of me and warning me not to walk in the way of the people: Call not alliance what this people calls alliance, and fear not, nor stand in awe of what they fear. (Isaiah 8:11)

Jonah's refusal to go to Nineveh strongly contrasts with the attitude of the Servant of the Lord described in Second Isaiah:

> The Lord God has given me a well-trained tongue,
> That I might know how to speak to the weary a word that will rouse them.
> Morning after morning he opens my ear that I may hear;
> And I have not rebelled, have not turned back.
> I gave my back to those who beat me, my cheeks to those who plucked my beard.
> My face I did not shield from buffets and spitting. (Isaiah 50:4-6)

This mysterious figure is, of course, a figure of Christ who will enter the Nineveh of this world and save us all by his life and word.

We can trace a progressive descent on Jonah's part. First he went down from the mountains of Palestine to the sea. Then he went down into the boat. Once in the boat, he went down to its bottom. The only form of further descent open to him then was into sleep, and this is just what he did. While all around him were praying and fighting the storm, Jonah was not only sleeping, but the Greek translation made in the closing centuries before Christ which we call the "Septuagint" adds that Jonah was snoring. The final descent followed when the sailors threw him overboard and he went down the whale's gullet. Then he was as close to Sheol, the region of the dead, as possible. The fact that throwing him over the side was his suggestion and not that of the crew, shows that Jonah would rather have been dead than go to Nineveh. He repeated the desire for death at the end of the book. He has appropriately been named the "recalcitrant prophet." He kicks against the goad even more than St. Paul.

Jonah did not argue with God. This is the worst thing about the way he refused his job; it was basically a refusal of dialogue. He simply received the command in silence and got up and went in exactly the opposite direction and to the point furthest from Nineveh. This is all the more serious when we reflect that, for the Bible, man is created for dialogue with God. In Genesis 2:18-21, man's distinctive privilege consists in his ability to respond to God's action by naming things. He is most human when he responds to God's gifts with his own word and with the gift of himself. For if the animals have eyes and ears, only man has the gift of language. There is only one term each in Hebrew to designate eyes and ears, but there is a whole series of words with different shades of meaning to designate the mouth. This shows us how essential the Hebrews regarded speech in man's existence. He is essentially a speaking being. Jonah knew that he would lose in any dialogue with God, so he didn't want to talk. His plan was not only not to go to Nineveh, but to get away from the very spot where he received the command. This would help him to get the whole thing off his mind.

If Jonah was trying to forget God, God was by no means going to forget his prophet. He was not going to force him to go to Nineveh. This would be contrary to the liberty with which he had endowed him. But he was going to use the events of Jonah's life, the whale included, to let him know that he should freely choose the path to Nineveh, and that his own freedom would increase to the extent that he conquered his lower nature, his feeling of hatred and revenge and opted for solidarity with God's plan, and with those to whom God was sending him. When St. Paul got up, after he had been knocked off his horse on the road to Damascus, he could have told himself that he had had enough of this religious business and that it was now time to take a wife and settle down to tent making. The fact that he acted otherwise was only the fruit of his free cooperation with the grace God was offering him. God incites us and stimulates us, but never forces us.

When the storm hit the ship Jonah was traveling in, the sailors threw everything overboard but the right thing. As St. Jerome remarks, they thought there was too much cargo, not realizing that the only surplus cargo was the prophet. Like Jonah himself, they were offering God everything except the one thing he really wanted.

Jonah's sleep on the boat could hardly be regarded as the sign of a tranquil conscience. It was rather a result of his exhaustion after his long trip. The same Hebrew word used to describe this deep sleep is also applied to the slumbers of another fugitive, Sisera, the general of the Canaanite army defeated by Deborah and Barak. This unfortunate man fled on foot to the tent of Jael, who offered him hospitality, gave him milk to drink and tucked him in bed. When he was sound asleep, she "got a tent peg and took a mallet in her hand . . . and drove the peg through his temple down into the ground, so that he perished in death." *(Judges 4:21)* Jonah fared better. He was awakened by a pagan sea captain who urged the Hebrew prophet to get up and pray! This was the second time in the book someone had asked Jonah to get up and do something. Both God and the captain got a negative response.

Jonah under his gourd was about to learn from God himself a little of the great message of St. John's Gospel: that God, in Christ, has come to lost and wandering man to enlighten him and so draw him out of the darkness created by his own blindness by offering him his love which, if accepted, will make him a loving person, freeing him from the inability to love inherent in all sin.

Jonah's solitude outside of Nineveh is a symbol of the isolation sin shuts man up in, not only oppressing his own being, but clipping the dynamism of his relation to others, a relation which constitutes human existence. Only when God's infinite love descended and picked Jonah up, and inserted him into its own dynamism, would Jonah begin to live again as a person, as a being who receives and gives love.

Even if Jonah were making merry in the best bar in Nineveh, surrounded by jovial Assyrian companions, he would still not be freed from his solitude as long as the Holy Spirit had not taken possession of his heart. For it is the Holy Spirit who saves man from the hell of solitude by bringing him into communion with the person of Christ, who is the only solid source and foundation of real communion among men.

Both Jonah and St. Paul started off in the wrong

direction, but there is a difference: Paul was seeking God where he wasn't, but Jonah wasn't seeking God at all. God went after both and corrected them: Jonah in the whale, Paul on the Damascus road. Both were building their lives on false foundations. St. Paul was looking for an existence based on the "law" in which God and man would be on equal footing. God would reward man's works and man would feel that they merited such a reward. Paul was after auto-affirmation and autonomy before God. He was locating the relation between God and man in the order of objects, i.e. law, rite, works, instead of in the new personal order inaugurated by Christ in which man exists as a son before God, accepting and returning his love, basing his existence on God's free grace and his gift of liberty and accepting a justification gratuitously bestowed by Christ's death. Jonah was trying to live without God. He was hoping to base his life on his own forces, on his own ability to forget God and take care of himself. Both were counterdistinguishing their liberty from that of God in a confrontation. This can only lead man to frustration and anguish, for he is only really free when he accepts the freedom Christ won for him and lives in complete dependence on, and in subordination to, the creative and sustaining liberty of God.

The fact that Jonah went to extremes in his self-assertion does not mean that the Christian should conclude that he must never affirm himself in the Church. For he is not a mere executor of tasks which oblige the collectivity and which can be performed by everybody indiscriminately. God is not like a stonemason who hacks and cuts his material to make it fit into the wall, as if only the wall and not the material too were all that he cared about. He has created everyone for an irreplaceable role in the Church and he can use anyone as a means for speaking to the whole community. Hence the community is not only an absolute for the individual, but in an analogous way the individual is in principle an absolute for the community. Every member has certain natural gifts and charisms from the Spirit which ordinarily indicate his vocation within the community. But in following that vocation, each one must listen to the criticisms and suggestions of the other members. He must be aware of the limitations every vocation implies and be ready for collaboration and dialogue with others.

If we rarely find people within the Church today as narrow-minded as Jonah, there are new forms of narrowness that can afflict us. If, for example, any group within the Church refuses to listen to others, rejects dialogue or communication and despises any suggestion of a critical revision of itself, we are faced with a collective Jonah. We have a movement away from Nineveh rather than toward God's will. And if, on the individual level, any Christian shuts himself off from dialogue with his brothers, proposing his own ideas and projects, his books and courses as the only ones really valid for the problems of the modern world, he is much closer to Jonah than to Christ. For the spirit of Jesus is one of broadness, liberty and trust before God, and this is just where it finds the source of its exigency. The Christian is relaxed and confident before his heavenly Father and so ready to go in any direction he is called, for he believes that God can save the modern Nineveh in more ways than one, especially than the particular one he has chosen to back.

The author of the book of Jonah identifies our hero with Jonah, son of Amittai, a prophet mentioned in 2 Kings 14:25, who lived in the northern kingdom of Israel during the middle of the eighth century. The Hebrew word *yonah* is both a proper name as well as a common noun meaning "dove."

It occurs quite often in the Old Testament and also has a metaphorical use in the Song of Songs where it becomes a term of endearment for the spouse or beloved girl described in that work, who is thrice referred to as "my dove." It is quite likely that when the author of Jonah looked around for a name to give his hero, he picked out Jonah partly because of the associations with a dove which it would arouse in the minds of his readers. For example, one of the psalms reads:

> And I say, Had I but wings like a dove,
>   I would fly away and be at rest.
> Far away I would flee;
>   I would lodge in the wilderness. (Psalm 55:7f)

Whether or not the references in the Song of Songs had any influence is another matter. Our author may not have known it. But for us today Jonah is certainly worthy of being showered with terms of endearment. Having been a favorite subject in Christian art, literature and preaching for some two thousand years, he is now more up-to-date than ever.

The Sign of Jonah

But the Lord sent a large fish, that swallowed Jonah; and he remained in the belly of the fish three days and three nights. (Jonah 2:1)

After the resurrection and descent of the Holy Spirit, when the apostles began to recollect Jesus' words and deeds, they had a very useful book to guide them in their effort at understanding him: the Old Testament. St. Paul expressed the first Christians' view of this book very well when he said: "Everything written before our time was written for our instruction." *(Romans 15:4)* For without this book, Christ would have been incomprehensible to them. It served as the stone quarry from which they drew the foundations which were to support the first Christian theological edifice. In this book they read the earlier history of man's encounter with God and with himself. They also found there an anticipated biography of Jesus written and lived by the psalmists, kings and prophets who fill its pages. One of these was Jonah. Jesus referred to him as a sign of his own death and resurrection. When the Pharisees asked to see some tangible sign of his mission, some sort of cosmic or astronomical disturbance, Jesus pointed to poor Jonah. He was worth a whole bag of cosmic signs.

There are two different interpretations of the sign of Jonah. In St. Luke, Jesus says: "Just as Jonah was a sign for the Ninevites, so will the Son of Man be a sign for the present age." *(Luke 11:30)* In other words, just as Jonah's appearance in Nineveh after his miraculous liberation from sure death in the whale's belly leaves no doubt that his mission was from God, so Jesus' own resurrection from death should mean the same thing to his incredulous audience. Jesus' words here could also mean that his message put before his audience before the necessity to decide for or against him, just as Jonah's had forced a decision on the Ninevites: conversion or destruction.

In his explanation of the sign of Jonah, St. Matthew stresses the fact that Jonah was saved from death. "Just as Jonah spent three days and three nights in the belly of the whale, so will the Son of Man spend three days and three nights in the bowels of the earth." *(Matthew 12:40)* As Jonah offered himself freely to save the sailors' lives and was saved by a miracle after three days and nights, Jesus now willingly offers his life for us and God will also save him. Thus Jonah's act symbolizes Jesus' voluntary sacrifice, his death and resurrection. And Jonah's preaching to the pagans, with its positive effect, will be a scandal for Jesus' incredulous Jewish audience. "At the judgment, the citizens of Nineveh will rise with the present generation and be the ones to condemn it. At the preaching of Jonah they reformed their lives; but you have a greater than Jonah here." *(Matthew 12:41)*

Jonah is a prototype of the Christian who, through the small deaths and renunciations that fidelity to God's will demand of him daily, becomes a witness to the power of the resurrection. If St. Paul described this as dying daily *(1 Corinthians 15:31)*, it can likewise be represented as a daily entering into the whale's belly.

The whale is a symbol of the instruments God uses to develop his divine life in us. The gourd is another such symbol and so is the worm. All three are described in the text as having been specially prepared by God for use on Jonah. If we lose the spirit of faith, we forget the great biblical lesson of instrumental causality which characterizes God's action in the world. In the book of Jonah we can see God acting on our hero through the storm, through the plant kingdom (the gourd), the animal kingdom (the whale) and through other men (the sailors). If we drop the spirit of faith, we are dealing with God only through his instruments, through the mediations behind which he hides in this life. For all creatures — mineral, plant, animal and man — have a double being: one according to their simple nature, another arising from their relation to God by which he can use them to mediate his presence and action in the world. The natural man sees only the first being. The man of faith sees both.

St. John of the Cross cites the Old Testament far more often than the New. Of the one thousand and sixty biblical quotations in his major works, we have six hundred and eighty-four from the Old and only three hundred and seventy-six from the New Testament. Thus two-thirds of the quotations are from the Old Testament. In both Testaments, St. John finds the same three constants: (1) a transcendent yet ever immanent God; (2) God's relation to man through Christ; and (3) the divine life in man. Both Testaments present him with the richest possible spiritual doctrine and experience incarnated in persons who lived closely united to

God. His preference for the Old Testament was due to the more abundant detailed descriptions of the interior life found there. In Job, Jeremiah, David (whom he considered as the author of the Psalms), and Jonah he found men who had passed through "the dark night" he was describing. Jonah's lodging in the whale's belly is an ideal image of man being purified in preparation for divine union. This "tomb of dark death" as St. John names it, is the proper place to await the spiritual resurrection every Christian longs for *(Dark Night 2, 6, 1)*. And he quotes Jonah's prayer in the midst of this tomb as an apt expression of the anguish of isolation during the purification process *(Ibid., 2, 6, 3)*.

We may sometimes think that the dark nights spoken of by St. John of the Cross is something that only happens to great saints. But God asked a man who was certainly no paragon of sanctity to go to Nineveh and thus placed him in the dark night. For St. John, the active night symbolizes our own efforts at self-purification, while the passive night is an image of the trials and sufferings which God brings into our life against our will or at least without consulting us. These are much more beneficial as they penetrate deeper into the soul. Every man's life has a large proportion of such passivities, of involuntary trials which place his life into a kind of darkness which St. John rightly calls a dark night. Most people do all they can to avoid them; this is only natural. But for those who have the faith to see God's action in them and to accept them, they become a great means of sanctification. We can sympathize with poor Jonah in his efforts to escape God's work on his soul. But at the same time we can learn from his failure to escape how much better it is to accept the passivities that are clearly God's will for us, as soon as they come, without forcing God to prepare a whale to bring us back to reason.

Jonah had a clear and direct call to enter the dark night. For most of us, however, the invitation is not so obvious. It will come through the duties of obedience or charity which come into our life. We will find that a great sacrifice is being asked of us in order to remain faithful to someone with whom our life is intertwined, or that a real demand is being made on our charity. This will be a direct challenge to the sincerity of our will to follow Christ and live as sons of God. Our own development as persons and as Christians will depend to a great extent on how we react. We can take a ship to Tarshish like Jonah, or we can go out to meet our cross with love and enthusiasm and try to incorporate it actively into our own program. This latter course was taken by St. Paul and Jesus himself. They had the flexibility to adjust to the new directions God's will pointed out to them, and to enter with love and trust into the painful passive situations it indicated.

One reason why painful passive situations are difficult to accept is that they are often caused by human mistakes or malice. We see that men are acting in them and producing them, but we fail to see that they are simultaneously God's touch upon us, God's action in our lives. When the sailors cast lots and Jonah's number came up, he had enough faith to see God working there as well as the seamen. This time he was able to adjust and incorporate the situation into his plans. He accepted the trial actively and came out of the whale a better man, a much closer friend of God.

The book's final irreplaceable scene shows Jonah dialoging with God and longing for death. He had undergone a deep humiliation which wounded his sensitivity. He felt let down. How could God do such a thing? His theology of salvation had been refuted by God himself. This may have hurt him more than anything else. The theology he had constructed with so much time and effort now lay shattered at his feet. The peace and joy it had given him by offering him a coherent vision of his faith and a clear understanding of all the ins and outs of his religion were now gone. He had to admit it — his theology was dead. He was not only depressed, he was very confused. He was, in fact, faced with a severe crisis of faith. What kind of a God was this and what theology was he following? Now Jonah would have to rethink the whole thing from the beginning. He would have to fit the Assyrians and their sort into his work and think through a whole new vision of divine mercy. His difficulty was quite similar to that of many Christians today. So much that they thought was a fixed part of their faith has turned out to be only an opinion or a false tradition. God is teaching them a new theology, his theology, through the events of history and the reflection of those events in the Church. These events are the whale's belly for them.

Jonah left Nineveh to watch the fireworks. He could time them to the day and even the hour. He sat in expectation, but not without a slight fear of disappointment, for he knew God could do strange things. As the end of the forty-day period drew near, Jonah was saying to himself, "Good-bye, Nineveh." But nothing happened. God had let him down. Like Jeremiah, he felt that God had seduced him, had led him into doing and promising things, and then had canceled the destruction. This feeling of deception may be one of the hardest trials many Christians have to bear today, one of their darkest nights. They followed what they thought was God's call and will, they were faithful in doing their duty, but the results they expected never followed. "You duped me, O Lord, and I let myself be duped; you were too strong for me, and you triumphed." *(Jeremiah 20:7)*

Jonah was very popular in early Christian art, no doubt because he was seen as a symbol of the resurrection of Christ and of the Christian. He was represented in several ways: being thrown into the whale's mouth, just emerging from it, as seated on the beach recovering from the ordeal, or finally as seated under his gourd outside of Nineveh. In almost all the man overboard scenes, Jonah is naked and being thrown into the fish by one of the sailors. He goes in head first with his hands stretched out in front as if diving. But he doesn't come out of the fish feet first, as should be expected, but head first again, perhaps to symbolize the metamorphosis which took place within the whale. One renaissance artist even portrays him entering naked and emerging fully clothed, as if there were some sort of clothing store in the whale's belly. This symbolizes his transformation from the old man and his deeds into the new man, vested in Christ.

The Koran tells us that if Jonah had not prayed while he was in the whale, he would still be there: "Jonah, too, was one of Our apostles. He fled to the laden ship, cast lots with the crew, and was condemned. A whale swallowed him, for he had done amiss; and had he not devoutly praised Allah he would have stayed in its belly till the Day of the Resurrection. We threw him, gravely ill, upon a desolate shore and caused a gourd-tree to grow over him. Thus We sent him to a nation a hundred thousand strong or more. They believed in him and We let them live in ease awhile." *(chapter 37)* Mohammed also thinks that God should forgive the Assyrians, for he puts these words into Allah's mouth: "Nor do We punish a nation until We have sent forth an apostle to warn them. . . . If they persist in sin, We rightly pass Our judgement and utterly destroy them." *(chapter 17)*

As could be expected, Jonah has his place in rabbinical literature. The rabbis claim that the fish which swallowed him had been created from the beginning of the world for just this purpose. Its mouth and gullet were so wide that Jonah had no problem making his way down. It was like passing through the doors of the widest synagogue. The whale's eyes were as big as windows and its interior was illuminated with lamps. Some of the rabbis also thought that there was a huge pearl hanging inside in which Jonah could see everything that took place in the sea. However, comfortable as he was, the good fish informed Jonah that this life could not go on forever, since he himself was about to be devoured by a still larger monster named Leviathan. Not at all daunted, Jonah asked the fish to take him immediately to Leviathan. When they drew near, Jonah showed the monster "Abraham's seal," which so frightened it that it put two days journey between itself and Jonah. As a reward for saving his life, Jonah's good whale took him on a guided tour of the sea. This included a side trip to the passage followed by the Israelites when they crossed the Red Sea, as well as an inspection of the pillars upon which the earth rests. It is not surprising that after three days and nights amid such regal comfort, Jonah never gave prayer a thought. So God decided to pass him to another fish where things would not be quite so nice. This change was also necessary in order to explain why, in the Hebrew text, in verse one of chapter two, the fish is masculine while in the next verse it is feminine. A pregnant female fish therefore came near Jonah's whale and told it that if Jonah did not come aboard her she would devour both Jonah and the fish. She supported her demand by orders from

God himself and when both fish asked Leviathan, he confirmed the order.

So Jonah had to move into new lodgings which, since the female had her offspring already developing within her, left Jonah with very little living space. This wasn't the only problem, but it proved to be enough to finally move the prophet to prayer. However, God did not deign to answer Jonah's prayer until he obtained the prophet's promise to capture Leviathan. When Jonah gave his word, the fish received the order from God to drop Jonah on the beach. When the crew from the boat saw this, they threw their idols overboard, went back to Joppa and submitted to circumcision.

One of the sources of much of St. Paul's renunciation was his delicacy in not scandalizing weaker Christians who would not understand his conduct. He avoided things he had a right to use just because they might create a problem for a poorly instructed fellow Christian *(1 Corinthians 8:13)*. Jonah didn't give a thought to how his conduct might affect others when he took ship for Tarshish. However, he began to come to his senses when the storm broke out and he saw that the sailors were suffering on his account. "Pick me up and throw me into the sea. . . . "

A glance at the map shows us that Nineveh is a long way from Palestine and that whoever went from one place to the other was in for plenty of hardship. Yet God sent Jonah to Nineveh. This symbolizes the necessary asceticism in every Christian life. Nobody can do anything worthwhile for God without some ascetical demand being made of him. The whale, of course, is a better symbol because it reveals how asceticism purges and corrects man's sinful tendencies which cause his flight from God. But both make us aware that asceticism is not something added to Christianity from the outside, but a part of its very substance.

Many Christians waste a large part of their energy because of their lack of personal discipline. If only Jonah had exercised more self-control when the Lord sent him to Nineveh the first time, how many useless footsteps and how much anguish he could have spared himself and others. Many neglect personal discipline, perhaps, with the thought that if their professional or apostolic work is well done they will be sufficiently disciplined. But this may mean that they are living on without really knowing themselves and are committing many faults which could have been checked by better interior observation and control. For the Bible, the heart is the conscience as well as the organ of understanding and volition. Hence we are asked to keep a close watch over it: "With closest custody, guard your heart, for in it are the sources of life." (Proverbs 4:23)

One reason for the low esteem into which asceticism has fallen today is a hangover from the past, when it was looked on as an isolated sector of Christian life which could be cultivated apart from a full Christian existence. This meant regarding Christian life itself as part of asceticism instead of asceticism as only one aspect of Christian life. It meant making Christ and the new life he brought us an instrument for the attainment of some ascetic ideal. It put the cart before the horse. Jesus and St. Paul show us the proper harmony between asceticism and the rest of Christian existence. The Christian is asked, primarily, to love God and his neighbor and to give witness to Christ and, only secondarily, to dominate his evil tendencies which can hinder that love and witness. Jonah well knew that his plunge into the sea would put real ascetical demands on him. But when he accepted it as the means necessary for the salvation of the sailors, he was acting like Jesus who accepted the Cross as the means of saving all of us.

In the Ninevites' penance we can see the classical forms of mortification then in use: fasting and sackcloth together with sitting on ashes. Today these would not have the same effect on us as they did on the Ninevites. We mature later than they did, we are more nervous than they were, and we suffer more intensely with less stimulant than they did. For us today there is also a greater underlying connection between pain and pleasure, including sexual pleasure, than in the days of Jonah. So new forms of mortification which really help us spiritually must be sought. The key word today is development rather than mortification. This is one result of the new theological vision of man and of the world accepted by so many Christians. But this should not lead us to despise or ridicule the Ninevites for not substituting social benefit programs for their fasting and ashes. If they had done so, Jonah might have had his fireworks after all.

Today many have an awful lot of confidence in the psychological studies of man and mortification which have been made. These can be very helpful, yet they are poor guides. They do not inspire us to follow Christ with his Cross. The Ninevites can show us the right road to the discovery of the forms of penance we need. They were first penetrated with a deep spirit of compunction and an inner desire for conversion. They then reached for the appropriate means of expressing these feelings. This is the right way: get the spirit first and then look for the means to express it.

Jesus didn't ask his followers to perform penetential exercises. He called for a real theological renunciation that goes much deeper than any practice we might inflict on our body. Bodily mortifications are only stimulants to keep us in shape for the really important sacrifices which our following of Christ may require. God did not ask Jonah to fast or to stand in cold water. He told him to go to Nineveh. This would have implied some fasting and hardship on the road, but they would have come as a by-product of his mission and not as isolated exercises, performed for themselves, separated from the rest of his life. St. Paul said that he died daily *(1 Corinthians 15:31)*, but most of the physical and moral privations which came into his life were met with in carrying out his mission. He left us two fine lists of them — 2 Corinthians 6:3-10 and 11:23-33 — against which we can examine our own lives.

If life in Jonah's day was uncertain and insecure, one reason was Palestine's geographical position on the royal road between two great world powers; human existence today has new forms of insecurity. The Church too is living through one of the greatest periods of change and uncertainty in her history and the tension implied in such an event adds to the stress of Christian life, and offers us a very real form of suffering. The growth of atheism, the difficulty millions of people have finding meaning in life, and the degradation experienced by so many in a life of depersonalized anonymity are all modern forms of mortification which the Christian must assimilate and whose poison he must counteract.

Since Jonah's passage through the whale is a symbol of Christ's death and resurrection, it is also a figure of a fundamental law in every Christian life: death to sin in order that Christ's life may grow in us. Death and resurrection are the two poles of Christian existence. They are found in Christ's life and must be present in that of the Christian. There is no union with God nor Christian maturity without them. They are as inseparable as the two sides of a coin: renunciation produces life. The seed dies and new life is born. The New Testament is very clear about our need for the Cross. We can see how essential it was in Jesus' life and how he made it a necessary condition for following him *(Mark 8:34ff)*. St. Paul both synthesized this doctrine and exemplified it in his own existence: "Continually we carry about in our bodies the dying of Jesus, so that in our bodies the life of Jesus may also be revealed." *(2 Corinthians 4:10)*

God's closing words to Jonah about the Ninevites, who don't know their right hand from their left, are used by St. John of the Cross to describe how our unmortified passions and appetites for created goods can spiritually blind us so that we cannot tell right from wrong *(Ascent 1, 8, 7)*. If Solomon, with his charismatic wisdom, fell into foolishness in his old age and became an idolater, all because he refused to control his passion for women, how great must be the darkness many of us live in who have no such gifts and yet have unmortified passions? This is St. John's point.

God loved the Ninevites and was already planning to send his Son to die for them. Christ's death is the center of St. Paul's theology. He saw this act not only as bringing salvation for the human race, but as individualized for each member of that totality. He says in Galatians 2:20 that Christ "loved me and gave himself for me." And in his discussions about avoiding scandal, he twice concluded his argument with the remark that we must not ruin "that brother for whom Christ died." *(Romans 14:15; 1 Corinthians 8:11)* Jonah never knew about that death. In it he would have discovered his own inauthenticity, his sin and its consequences, but he would also have found there the power he needed to authenticate his existence, to begin to serve God by a new life. He would have realized Christ's love for himself and for each of the Ninevites he so hated.

Christ's Cross, in St. Paul's mind, is an invitation for man to abandon his false self-understanding based on "boasting," and to accept a new one founded on charity. It calls on all Jonahs to become aware of just where their trip to Tarshish is leading them — to death — and incites them to seek reconciliation with God, putting their vanities and illusions aside and forming a new existence based on the authenticity of grace and charity.

In many ways the book of Jonah anticipates the parable of the Prodigal Son. St. Paul's epistle to the Romans is also a personal commentary on this gospel story. He shows us what happens to man when he seeks his best being, his life and his justification in realities inferior to himself. He points out how man's only real home, the only place where he can regain his authenticity, is the Cross of Christ. This is the Father's house, the place where God's love is most manifest. Any attempt by man to find his justification elsewhere is doomed to failure. Jonah sought justification through his membership in God's chosen people. In St. Paul's time many looked for it there too as well as in philosophical wisdom, the asceticism of the ethical religions and in the mystery cults. Today's temptations may be offered by advanced technology and expanded sciences of man such as psychology and anthropology. Man can feel he no longer needs God to found and to develop his life and to understand himself. As St. Paul said of the pagans of his day: "They claimed to be wise, but turned into fools instead." (Romans 1:22)

Jonah Prays
and Christian Prayer

From the belly of the fish Jonah said this prayer to the Lord, his God. (Jonah 2:2)

The text just quoted marks the turning point in the story of Jonah. Prayer is the crossroad where all Jonah's problems converge and find expression. He saw how futile his flight was, how cowardly it was, how much he was under the influence of unconscious drives and all the trouble it caused the sailors, who lost their cargo. Having repented of all this and made ready to amend, Jonah turned to God for the first time in the story and spoke in humble prayer. Even though we do not know the content of his prayer — since the psalm given in the text seems to be a later addition — we can be sure that it possessed all the qualities of authentic biblical prayer, since God heard it and had Jonah put on the beach. In our own lives, prayer often marks a turning point when we pull ourselves together in God's presence and make a new start. Jonah is something unheard of in prophetic history: a true (not a false) prophet who disobeyed God. In doing so he has proved to be a tremendous source of courage for those of us who have done the same thing. If he was able to change, so can we and in the same way: by prayer.

The people of Israel were born and raised in a climate of prayer. They lived in constant dialogue with God. The content of this dialogue was God's salvific plan and its multiple realizations in Israel's life. The main themes of Israel's prayer were, accordingly, the high points of salvation history: the election, the exodus, the desert period, the alliance, the conquest and the exile, etc. The quintessence of Israel's prayer is, of course, the Psalter. There both nature and history are given voice in man's praise and thanksgiving, in his petition and lament. Jonah's prayer in the whale's belly is thus quite rightly presented as an assortment of phrases from the Psalms. It is composed of a tiny anthology of such phrases which the prayer's author thought most appropriate for the occasion. It shows us that in our hours of need we don't have to reach for a ready-made psalm, but may find it easier to take scattered verses from several which the Holy Spirit brings to mind.

Jonah's prayer in the fish's belly has awakened the scholars' interest. They point out that it is not the sort of prayer we should expect. Instead of a plea for forgiveness or for deliverance from danger, Jonah sings a canticle of thanksgiving. Besides, there are several phrases in the psalm which do not quite square with Jonah's circumstances. There is also no mention of the good whale. The commentators then notice that, if we remove the psalm, we can see that verses two and eleven fuse together perfectly: " . . . Jonah said this prayer to the Lord, his God (and) then the Lord commanded the fish. . . . " So it seems that some later writer, not content with the beautiful little story as he found it, decided to give us the prayer's content. It is of course inspired like every part of the Bible and has its value, but it lacks the charm and simplicity of the rest of the book. The important thing, however, is that Jonah's self-sufficiency is finally shaken and he turns to prayer. He can no longer refuse to dialogue with his only source of life and salvation. His long silence is broken.

That psalm fragments should have been chosen to make up Jonah's prayer should not surprise us. The Bible has a natural relation to prayer. Prayer is, in fact, the best atmosphere in which to read the Scriptures, and they in turn provide prayer with its best nourishment. Jonah had grown up with the psalms and sacred writings embedded in his memory. It was only to be expected that at the hour of his crisis these texts should come to his lips. However, there is more than a mere memory mechanism involved here. Jonah's prayer is primarily a gift of the Holy Spirit. For even in a situation as desperate as Jonah's, when it would seem that there is after all nothing else the poor man can do but turn to prayer as a last straw before he blacks out, prayer is still one of God's greatest gifts. Even in our worst moments, it is the Holy Spirit who "helps us in our weakness" and "makes intercession for us with groanings that cannot be expressed in speech." *(Romans 8:26)*

The fact that Jonah's prayer was a gift should not obscure its solid human reality. Prayer calls for human effort. It is work. It demands a concentration of the whole man, interior and exterior faculties, that few if any other human actions can equal. The mind must be attentive to God, the will must intend to address him, and the imagination and the rest of the body must at least be kept from hindering the prayer if they cannot be brought in to help it. As one of the Desert Fathers expressed it years after Jonah's death: "Pardon me, but I think there is no greater effort than that required to pray to

God. Every time a man wants to pray, his enemies try to stop him. For they know that they will not hinder his progress unless they can get him away from prayer. Whatever good a man undertakes, if he perseveres in it he will have peace. But in the case of prayer, he will have to fight until his last breath."

Jonah's real prayer in the whale's belly no doubt anticipated a form of prayer that is becoming quite popular today: situation prayer. This prayer, as the name suggests, springs from the particular situation the praying individual is living through and from which it takes its content and form of expression. Some examples of such situations might be a journey, a job, a very painful or very happy event, an important meeting, the beautiful scenery, a personal tragedy, a feast, etc. This type of prayer does not require the interiority, the fixed attention and mental effort needed in formal prayer. It is practical, brief and to the point. It does demand, however, the ability to sense the special spiritual meaning of the particular situation — a meaning that others may only see years later when they look back on the event. This prayer is made up of the details, persons and happenings of the situation itself. It is not composed outside the situation and dragged in. Thus it is more original than the traditional "ejaculatory" prayer, having more flexibility and depth since it is handmade to fit the circumstances. Jonah certainly had all the material for a real situation prayer, but the formal composition that has been put in his mouth by a later author bears the marks of a stranger introduced from outside. The brief fragment of Jonah's petition for death at the end of the book is a fine example of a tiny situation prayer.

Outside Nineveh, and standing beside his dead gourd, Jonah had everything he needed to put together a beautiful situation prayer. He had loved that plant and the sight of the withered remains lying at his feet should have reminded him that there is a worm in every gourd during this earthly pilgrimage. It should have made him reflect that we cannot depend on any created thing for our happiness, for the meaning and inspiration of our life. The very frequent biblical image of God as man's rock should have risen up in his mind as a striking contrast to the instability of his gourd. It has been said that the primary attribute of God grasped by man is not one of the more complex ones such as infinite, necessary or perfect, but his fundamentality. We first sense God as the foundation of all things and of ourselves. If we can believe the note in the Hebrew text which introduces Psalm 18, it arose as a kind of situation prayer: " . . . when the Lord had rescued (David) from the grasp of all his enemies and from the hand of Saul." David begins by a reference to God's fundamentality:

I love you, O Lord, my strength,
*   O Lord, my rock, my fortress, my deliv-*
*   erer.*
My God, my rock of refuge,
*   my shield, the horn of my salvation, my*
*   stronghold!*

He then refers to the situation:

Praised be the Lord, I exclaim,
*   and I am safe from all my enemies.*

Jonah, in his own situation, could have composed something like the first part, but he would have to include a petition for deliverance from attachment to his gourd rather than thanksgiving as his conclusion, for poor Jonah was firmly tied to his plant.

If Jonah really loved his gourd, so did the early Christians. They painted it on their tombs with Jonah seated under it. We find, for example, such a representation in the Cemetery of St. Callistus in Rome. Perhaps what they saw in Jonah's gourd was a symbol of the vanity of life, which springs up and dies with the speed of a plant. With so many people living today as if they thought they were going to be here forever, renewed interest in this aspect of Jonah may help us all. For whoever is not able to live at ease with death, will be its victim. And instead of accepting it with love and preparing for it with faith, he will fall trembling with fear into its hands. But without prayer, no one can psychologically preserve a sense of the reality of God from whom he has received his life as a gift which must be returned with love.

Jonah's gourd caused quite a problem in the fourth-century Church. In one African see, Oea, the New Latin translation of Jonah just made by St. Jerome was read before the congregation for the first time. Everything went smoothly until the reader came to Jonah's gourd. Then a real brawl broke out. For Jerome had translated the Hebrew word *kikayon*, which even today is not identified with certainty but which may be a castor-oil plant or a species of cucumber or gourd, by "ivy." There were quite a few Greeks among the group and these, especially, but the others also were used to the old Greek Septuagint translation "gourd." St. Augustine tells St. Jerome by letter what happened: "Such a great tumult broke out in the congregation, especially among the Greeks who shouted that it was a calumny, that the bishop was obliged to consult the Jews. They answered, I don't know if by ignorance or by malice, that what was in the Hebrew codices was what the Latins and

Greeks had said. And what followed? The good man saw himself obliged to correct the error, desiring after such great danger, not to be left without any people." The scandal reached Rome where St. Jerome was accused of sacrilege for having translated ivy instead of gourd. Today we have learned to adjust to the new translations with less passion, but perhaps one reason for this is that we just don't have the Bible worked into our minds and hearts as the fourth-century Christians did. And this lack of grounding in the Bible is one reason why we may find it hard to pray.

As Jonah sat under his gourd outside of Nineveh waiting to see, as he hoped, the city destroyed, he may have engaged in some deep meditation. He may have thought over his own response to God's word, how defective it had been at first, but how too he had pulled himself together in the whale. He may also have tried to anticipate and brace himself for a possible disappointment in the future, for he knew how mysterious God was and that he must be ready for anything. He should have come forth from this meditation with a greater sense of God and a deeper penetration into his plans. But perhaps he didn't meditate. Perhaps he just waited the time out, and this is why he responded so poorly when the city was spared. The very ancient biblical practice of meditation, which as Psalm 1 says makes a man "like a tree planted near running water, that yields its fruit in due season, and whose leaves never fail," should never be omitted in Christian life. It is an integral part of prayer and keeps it from becoming pure feeling or affection with no real roots in thought. Without meditation man's noblest faculty, his intellect, is eliminated from his life of prayer.

If Jonah's meditation under his gourd was really biblical, it was a prolonged loving reflection on

God and his mystery. It implied the presence of the mystery of Christ, which was already developing under the ancient alliance. It took in God's dealing with Israel and with the Assyrians. It turned quite naturally into a dialogue with God, into formal prayer, even though the prayer was a petition for his own death. Thus meditation is the normal preparation for prayer which, like any serious act of the whole person, cannot be begun without some form of recollection and thought. This reflection is intended to be a means of assimilating the object meditated on into our thought, heart and activity. It is already a first step or moment of prayer and must never be left out of our life. Rather than a practice for beginners only, it usually takes a very mature Christian to make a real meditation.

It might seem to be going too far to speak of contemplation in the book of Jonah, but its closing chapter presents us with the essentials of contemplative prayer: a loving simple turning to God, a simple loving knowledge of God, which is how St. John of the Cross defines contemplation. *(Living Flame of Love 3:34)* This knowledge may either have been the fruit of Jonah's meditation or it may have been infused. The fact that this contemplation includes a petition for his own death is no argument against its authenticity. We cannot judge Jonah in the light of a gospel he never heard. He was still living in the relative obscurity of the Old Law where a desire for death in circumstances such as his was quite understandable. Job and Jeremiah longed for the same thing. Many a modern Jonah will find himself in a psychological state very similar to Jonah's, not because of his disappointment with God's mercy, but due to the inner poverty and darkness that can follow after a day of very heavy work or after some exhausting form of service. He will only be able to pray with a simple loving glance at God. This can be called the prayer of pure faith, the prayer of silence or of presence, or perhaps simply adoration.

Both Jonah and the Christian are called to exercise an apostolate. This apostolate is not, strictly speaking, a part of prayer although it is not unrelated to prayer. The soul of the modern apostolate is not prayer but charity. The purpose of this apostolate is to build up God's kingdom. It is a part of every Christian's life whether he prays or not. It is demanded by his fidelity to Christ and can become a means for his own sanctification as well as that of others. We can see this in Jonah's life. The apostolate presupposes some experience of God to which the apostle bears witness, but it does not necessarily require a mature life of prayer. Rather than a fruit of prolonged prayer, it may lead the Christian to take prayer seriously, just as Jonah's apostolic experience stimulated him to prayer. Thus prayer and apostolic activity go together and must harmonize in every life. If Jonah's form of apostolate, i.e. missionary work aimed at the conversion of pagans and the spread of God's kingdom, is the principal one, it is by no means the only type of apostolic activity. Many will be engaged in cultivating the Christian life of those already converted. Each of us has to contribute something or we are not a really living member of the Church. We are, instead, running off to Tarshish.

Jonah beside his dead gourd, if only he knew it, was in an ideal position for union with God. He had been stripped of everything. His country, family, and his gourd were gone, and even his ideas were discarded by God himself. If only Jonah would let go of them, he would be able to await, in faith and trust, God's coming to him in a more personal and loving manner than ever before. Once Jonah was free from all his passions and evil inclinations, union with God would follow. There is an infallible link between man's emptiness and the infusion of God's life. But if Jonah was going to hold onto his false ideas and continue to let his passions dominate his life, what could God do?

Jonah had plenty of solitude and silence in his hut outside Nineveh, but these by themselves are only means for union with God. The material solitude he was enjoying had to be completed by an interior spiritual solitude, by a deep desire to have God as his closest friend. This spiritual solitude will go hand in hand with a need for inner silence. Jonah had to learn to be near God in the attitude of a listener, with his passions, mind and imagination stilled. This silence is more than mere lack of words. It is something positive. It is an interior fullness, for God is then speaking to man in the best of all languages: the language of love.

Jonah's Apostolate and Ours

The word of the Lord came to Jonah a second time: "Set out for the great city of Nineveh, and announce to it the message that I will tell you." So Jonah made ready and went to Nineveh, according to the Lord's bidding. (Jonah 3:1-3)

Jonah's miraculous liberation from the whale in some way founded his mission to the Ninevites, just as Jesus' resurrection acts as the foundation for the apostles' mission. The resurrection made those who had been Jesus' disciples become his messengers. Jesus' appearances to his apostles, after his resurrection, strengthened and confirmed their faith and gave birth to the Christian missions. When the Holy Spirit descended on Pentecost, those missions were actually launched. For just as Jonah needed a new impulse from God when he lay on the beach where the whale had placed him, so the apostles had to receive the Spirit's power and direction before they could move and preach to all men.

Jonah was sent to the pagans. He was thus a prototype of the Christian missionary. He was not an ideal missionary, of course, because he did not go willingly. The Christian doesn't go to the pagans because he is afraid they will be condemned if they die without having heard the gospel, because their eternal fate is something he knows nothing about and which depends upon God and the individual. The Christian goes to the missions because he realizes the value of the life brought by Christ, and can only express his appreciation and joy for having that life by inviting other men to share it. He differs from Jonah too by the fact that his interest in the pagans is motivated by love. Jonah went hoping to see his detested audience wiped out. The Christian goes praying and hoping that his dearly loved pagan brothers will want to participate in the light and love that have gladdened his own existence.

Jesus acts out the message of the book of Jonah: He goes to sinners with love and concern because God does so too, because God is infinite love and concern for man. So we must accept the image of God which Jesus presents to us if we want to be his followers. And we must accept Jesus' conduct as the ideal and exemplary behavior, as the conduct that God wants us to imitate. Thus we must learn to see Jonah and all the other parts of the Bible as offering us sides or dimensions of the one, living, personal God to whom our final word must always be one of invocation: "Abba, Father."

The Parable of the Two Sons in St. Matthew's Gospel offers us a parallel with Jonah *(Matthew 21:28-31)*. The elder son said he would go and work in his father's vineyard, but he didn't go. The younger son at first said no, but then changed his mind and went. The younger son practiced true fidelity. It is true that it is a retarded fidelity, but it is real. In fact, it may even be firmer than that of many who said they would work and actually did, but whose fidelity has never been probed and tested. The younger son's surrender may not have been easy, but it was very solid. The essential thing in every vocation is not so much when we go to Nineveh, but the fact that we do go and deliver our message. The salvation of our modern world depends on just how many Jonahs are going to finally give in to divine love.

The Christian's primary mission is not insertion in the world but immersion in God. His insertion in the society of his day will only be fruitful, for the real growth of God's kingdom, if he is personally immersed in the mystery of God and in Christ. If Jonah had not been immersed in God, he would have had no message from God to speak when he got to Nineveh. If there was a tendency in the past for Christians to avoid their necessary insertion in the world, today the danger is that they become not inserted but submerged in the modern world. This can happen if they become so preoccupied about being regular fellows among the children of this world that they practically disappear as witnesses to Christ. If Jonah had tried to pass for just another Assyrian with nothing special on his mind, he would have ruined the mission he was sent on. He was to bear witness to God among these pagans and to deliver his message to them. He was to be a presence of God among them, not an absence.

Just as Jonah was primarily God's witness in Nineveh, the Christian's first duty today is to be the same thing. His first attention should be directed to living before God in faith, to knowing and loving him in pure disinterested service. And he should not look for any concrete results on the human level for this relation; it is completely unproductive and uninterested in historical effectiveness. But without this personal relation to God — a relation more deeply personal than that possible between two merely human persons — the Christian would be subjecting God to some further end. He would be making God a means for his own service to humanity. If this would not be legitimate in his relations with any other person, how much less proper is it in his communion with God.

If the Christian's primary interest is not God, he is in danger of turning God into an idol. He could act just like the Assyrian who worshiped Assur so that he could win more victories over his enemies. So the Christian apostle must aim at letting the mystery of Christ shine forth in his life with no eye to how he may appear on this world's stage. His prime duty is to God and he will only please men when doing so is part of his service of God. This is the only way he can keep his witness from being influenced and dimmed by other people's desires. If Jonah had not been living primarily before God, he might have preached quite a different message in Nineveh. It might have run something like this: "Yahweh, my God, would like to see some changes made here. I realize that Assur, your god, and Ishtar, his spouse, may feel that this is cutting in on their territory. Now if that's the case, well let's try to work out some middle path between what you are doing now — which greatly displeases my God — murders, blinding of prisoners, impalement of your enemies, etc., and a more, shall we say, moderate course in this whole business. For a start, how about depriving prisoners of only one eye in the future, and limiting rape, murder and the ripping of pregnant women to three days a week?" But this wouldn't work. Jonah simply couldn't serve two masters.

Jesus told his disciples that they should expect the world's hatred. He warned them that "they will harry you as they harried me." *(John 15:20)* He had done so many good and useful things for the people he lived among, although he was well aware that his mission was much more than that. But once he broached the subject of his real mission, the attitude of his audience changed: hostility, hatred and indifference met him everywhere. A Christian would be kidding himself if he thought he would find things different today. Once he shows that he is not just another social worker, he finds backs turned and doors shut. When he sets foot in Nineveh he has to be clear on why he is there and what to expect. This is where Jonah can help him.

St. Paul is an excellent example of the messenger's fidelity to the one who sent him. "Men should regard us as servants of Christ and administrators of the mysteries of God. The first requirement of an administrator is that he prove trustworthy. It matters little to me whether you or any human court pass judgment on me." *(1 Corinthians 4:1ff)* Jonah was certainly not tempted to a false compassion for his audience, but today's Christian may be. It could lead him to mutilate the gospel and forget that it is not his own message but Christ's. As long as the messenger is faithful to his Lord, he can count on divine power to support him. But once he begins preaching his own ideas, he will be at his audience's mercy. Jonah didn't entirely agree with the message he was told to preach in Nineveh. He would have liked to add to it something like: "Even if you Ninevites repent and perform every penance in the book, you will none the less be completely destroyed. Amen." Sometimes too St. Paul lets us know that the gospel message was not easy for him to deliver to persons whom he realized would be hurt by it in some way. He asks the Galatians: "Have I become your enemy just because I tell you the truth?" *(Galatians 4:16)* But he did tell them the truth.

If St. Paul is a paradigm or pattern of apostolic existence, of a life entirely dedicated to building up the Church, Jonah is an excellent example of a man who doesn't want to get involved any more than he has to. It is true that Jonah endured something for the Lord, but what did he suffer in comparison with Paul's tribulations: "Five times at the hands of the Jews I received forty lashes less one; three times I was beaten with rods; I was stoned once, shipwrecked three times; I passed a day and a night on the sea. . . . " *(2 Corinthians 11:24ff)* The great apostle has left us lists of his sufferings which make it clear how much the apostolic life cost him. Yet he sees all of this as merely the natural unfolding and development, in his existence, of the new life given to him by Christ. This is the death dimension in Christian life which brings with it a greater life dimension. The apostolic life implies a participation in Christ's death and resurrection.

The author of the book of Jonah wanted to make communion with God possible for even his people's enemies. He didn't ask that they accept circumcision and become Jews. He only invited them to obey the natural law inscribed in their hearts. He didn't even storm against idolatry, because he knew that they were not able to believe explicitly in the true God who had revealed himself to Israel. The Church today must learn how to incorporate into itself the great masses of the poor and uncultured people whom Jesus indicated as especially prepared to accept his message, while at the same time not allowing membership in the Church to be identified with belonging to any particular social or racial group. The faith must depend on personal decision and not on the race or social class to which one belongs. But a new circumcision in the form of western culture, philosophy and theology must not be imposed on them.

The gospel must never become the possession of an aristocratic minority who because of their wealth, culture or blood have easy access to it.

When Jonah's preaching had the effect he feared and God spared Nineveh, he became very depressed. He lacked the fortitude to endure the breakdown of his project and the destruction of his gourd. Today Jonah is a very common type. There are more apostles these days capable of launching projects and sacrificing for them as long as they succeed, than those who can peacefully survive the failure of their plans and programs. There is more dynamism around than fortitude, even though the latter is the superior quality.

To go to Nineveh, Jonah had to have faith in himself. He had to believe that he really had something to say when he got there and that it was worth listening to. He had to have faith in his message. This faith in the power and validity of the gospel message is vitally important for the modern Jonah. He must never doubt the power of the words he has to speak. He must realize that his words are supported by and often even supplied for by the infinite power of God, whose messenger he is.

The Christian's capacity for fruitful insertion in the world will be in proportion to the depth of his personal relation with God in faith and love. For unless he remains the salt of the earth through his union with Christ, he will have nothing to offer the modern Nineveh that couldn't be found equally well in numerous social movements. Therefore St. Paul warns his Christians not to be conformed to this world *(Romans 12:2)*, because unless they can preserve their own inner liberty from the chains and drives of the world, they can do nothing lasting for God's kingdom by their work in it.

The source of the modern Jonah's confidence in

his message is the Holy Spirit. For during the period between the two comings of Christ — the Incarnation, in the days of Pontius Pilate and the parousia at the end of history — it is the Spirit who fills history with salvific efficacy. But this Spirit first frees man himself from the power of sin which seeps into him through the weak and fallible element in his nature, the flesh, and flows into his will where it sets in motion a conflict between his desire to do good and his ability to carry out that desire *(Romans 7:8)*. The Holy Spirit resolves this conflict, restoring man to his lost unity and liberty and enabling him, in imitation of Jesus, to call God his father. He is then ready to speak to the modern Nineveh fully aware of the limits imposed on him by his own poverty, but also completely conscious of the harmony between his own being and that of the Spirit which gives him his life and the words he is uttering.

By the very fact that one is a Christian he is also an apostle. This is very clear in St. Paul's life, for his conversion coincides with his mission *(Acts 9:6)*. Jonah's life, as his book presents it, begins with a mission. For everyone there is some task of construction, conservation or development of the Church. No one is unemployed. Forms of apostolate vary from person to person and from time to time in the same person's life. After Jonah went home with his work in Nineveh completed, he may have exercised some other form of apostolate. He may have felt that prophetic work was a little too much for him after his ordeal, but there was plenty he could do in the more modest apostolate practiced by the father of a family. He may not have been able to do much more. In any case, there was no reason for him to feel that his work was done. There is no exemption from the apostolate, even for those who can do no more than offer the all-important service of prayer and suffering.

If Jonah at first lacked the prime quality of every apostle, fidelity, he later made up for his former weakness. He seems to have had plenty of the second gift needed by every apostle — sensitivity to others. Even if he didn't go as far as St. Paul in this and become all things to all men in order to save them *(1 Corinthians 9:22)*, yet he knew how to make the shoe fit in his address to the Ninevites. He understood enough of their socio-economic conditions, their national and racial characteristics to get his message across. In fact, he brought about an instant conversion that would have been enough to make the ordinary missionary strongly tempted to pride. But Jonah's anger and depression at the city's change of heart show that his sensitivity was not the fruit of real love. It was just part of his knack for bringing off a smooth job because he had to.

If charity was far from being the soul of Jonah's apostolate, his mission certainly provided him with a lesson in love. He got more out of it than he put in. He learned from the whole bitter experience that God is really all he had thought: he is merciful beyond reason and measure. In fact, he is so merciful that there is even room in that mercy for a narrow-minded and hateful prophet like himself. On his way back to Palestine some of this lesson no doubt began to sink in. The greatest conversion at Nineveh may well have been his.

Jonah's tendency to go his own way and live independent of God might have led him to become an apostolic "sharpshooter," i.e., a preacher who uses his capacity as God's representative as a sort of springboard to diffuse his own ideas. He would preach Nineveh's destruction all right, because he himself wanted it destroyed. But if he had yielded to his temptation, he would also have preached against the Ninevites' conversion so that God's plan would be frustrated and the destruction achieved. He would then have deformed God's message and been preaching his own. Fortunately he wasn't that bad.

It is just possible that mixed in with Jonah's refusal to undertake the form of apostolic work the Lord asked of him was the feeling that he was really superior to such a job. He may not only have hated the Assyrians, but also felt that preaching in a mission spot like Nineveh was beneath his dignity. It is quite possible that he had been formed in a prophetic school. We know from the books of Samuel and Kings that the prophetic institution was well developed in Israel. Jonah may have studied in some sort of Israelite Institute of Prophecy and Priestcraft from which he emerged with a degree in destructive prophecy: the famous B.D.P. degree. There would be, of course, a nice position open to him in his own country. Why should he go on the missions? He had an excellent career waiting for him in Samaria or perhaps in the Southern Kingdom. Hence his training, his greater capacity for his work, his degree, had really put him in a state of unavailability for anything he considered not quite up to his level. Instead of preparing him to be a better apostle, it created an obstacle to his apostolate. Before he went to I.I.P.P. and came out with his B.D.P. he had been ready to go anywhere and do any type of work asked of him. But now. . . .

If we want to avoid slipping into a disdain for forms of apostolic work which we consider beneath us, we have to grasp the new and broadened notion of the apostolate emphasized by Vatican II. Every function in the Christian community is a real apostolic mission. Washing floors, cooking, answering the door or the phone are all services to the community which, if done with love, very definitely build up the Kingdom of God and help others to grow in the knowledge and love of Christ. Jonah's narrowing of the field of apostolic activity to the type of work he liked had nothing prophetic and, a fortiori, nothing Christian about it.

If the apostolate is really a mutual service in love which Christians carry out in order to build up the Mystical Body and to spread the knowledge and love of Christ, no one is excluded from it and no one takes on any form of superiority from exercising it. It is a mutual, reciprocal service which all must take part in. As St. Paul said: "Yet preaching the gospel is not the subject of a boast; I am under the compulsion and have no choice. I am ruined if I do not preach it!" *(1 Corinthians 9:16)* One of Jonah's problems was that he didn't carry out his mission with love. He was an apostle who despised his audience, who regarded himself as above them, as their master rather than their servant.

Jonah ends up all alone under his gourd. He doesn't seem to have been invited to anyone's home or to have attracted any disciples or friends at Nineveh. What a contrast to St. Paul! But there is nothing surprising about Jonah's lack of friends. He lacked the love that forms friendships.

St. Paul tells us that in Asia he was crushed beyond his strength, even to the point of despairing of life *(2 Corinthians 1:8)*. But how different his reaction is to that of Jonah in the same condition. Paul saw his situation as a means of learning how to trust in God, who raises the dead, and not in himself: "He rescued us from that danger of death and will continue to do so. We have put our hope in him who will never cease to deliver us." *(verse 10)*

If Jonah wished he were dead, he still didn't do anything to kill himself. Job also longed for death:

Oh that I might have my request, and that God would grant what I long for: Even that God would decide to crush me, that he would put forth his hand and cut me off! (Job 6:8-9)

So did Jeremiah:

Cursed be the day on which I was born. . . . Why did I come forth from the womb, to see sorrow and pain, to end my days in shame? (Jeremiah 20:14ff)

Suicide, however, was very rare in Israel. The most detailed case is perhaps that of Ahithophel, the counselor, who when Absolam rejected his advice:

. . . saddled his ass and departed, going to his home in his own city. Then, having left orders concerning his family, he hanged himself. (2 Samuel 17:23)

Jonah saw God put his opinion aside and let his destruction project fail, but he still retained enough trust in the Lord not to look on the gourd-tree as a good place to hang himself.

In the Second Epistle to the Corinthians St. Paul has left the record of his own limit-experience, that is, which he had been unable to assimilate during his apostolic life. He called it "a thorn in the flesh." Just what the exact nature of this personal problem was is not certain. However, it made St. Paul touch bottom spiritually and realize that it was more than he could handle alone. After three attempts at being delivered from it through prayer, he received the answer from Christ: "My grace is enough for you, for in weakness power reaches perfection." *(2 Corinthians 12:9)* This taught Paul to not only tolerate his problem, to live with it, but to even rejoice in it in order, as he says, "that the power of Christ may rest upon me." Jonah didn't as yet understand this law of every apostolate. He may have come to see later on that his special thorn in the flesh, i.e. his false independence, his hatred and other uncontrolled passions could become a real springboard for union with God and with himself.

St. Paul received another lesson in the art of the Christian apostolate when he preached before the philosophers at Athens *(Acts 17)*. His strategy was fine. He would begin from where his audience stood as professional philosophers, and then lead them along the same path until they met Christ. But the sermon fell flat. No one was convinced. Or rather, the only one convinced was Paul himself. He was sure then that his logic and erudition alone were not going to do the job. We find him shortly after at Corinth preaching quite differently. Paul, then, was able to learn from his failures. He could ride punches and bend to situations. Jonah just collapsed and wished he were dead.

St. Paul felt a real spiritual compulsion to preach Christ. He felt he would be ruined if he did not proclaim the gospel *(1 Corinthians 9:16)*. Jonah's compulsion was to flee from preaching. Today there are perhaps more Jonahs around then Pauls. But this indicates a real weakness in the Church, for only by constantly thinking and speaking of Christ can we keep what he should mean and be for us alive and really make his teaching effective in our lives. We assimilate Christ by thinking about him, and by communicating him to others we become more deeply rooted in him ourselves. It would be a mistake to dedicate one's self completely to apostolic activity and leave aside all questions about Christ's meaning and his influence on the world. The content of our belief in Christ must be tangible to ourselves and communicable to others or it will soon cease to exercise any influence on us or on the world we move in.

In Jonah God had proven beyond any doubt that he is omnipresent, and therefore no man can flee from him. St. Matthew's Gospel ends with Jesus proclaiming a new form of God's omnipresence, which from now on will include an omnipresence of Christ: "And know that I am with you always, until the end of the world." For this reason Matthew makes no reference to an Ascension or disappearance of Jesus, since Jesus has rather become interiorized in human history, endowing it from within with his Spirit and from without with his apostles' word. As the angel had told Joseph at the beginning of Matthew's Gospel, Jesus will be called "Emmanuel, a name which means 'God is with us.'" *(Matthew 1:23)* Therefore the modern Jonah can go about his mission with a new assurance. For if everyone called to some special mission in the Old Testament was reinforced by God's promise to be with him (Abraham, Moses, Joshua, Gideon, David, Jeremiah, etc.), Jesus' promise goes further. He will not only be with his apostles, in so far as they are individuals sent on a mission for the people of God in the same way as Jonah was sent to Nineveh, but will also be with them as the heads of the new Israel, i.e. his presence will now extend to the totality of the Christian community. Every Christian now has the same assurance as the great leaders and prophets of the Old Testament that God, in Christ, will be with him in carrying out his specific apostolic task.

Christ's new promised presence to his followers on their missions also includes a new form of God's presence among men in personal intimacy. It thus prevents the Christian from living with a God who only acted in the past and turns his existence into an ongoing participation in God's own personal mystery and action in the world. If Matthew opened his gospel with a promise of Christ's saving presence, he closes it by concentrating that presence in the apostles' missionary activity and in Jesus' new interior dwelling in all Christians. Thus Jesus is already present and acting in history and therefore beginning to bring it to its close.

Nineveh's Conversion
and Ours

> *Jonah began his journey through the city,*
> *and had gone but a single day's walk announc-*
> *ing, "Forty days more and Nineveh shall be*
> *destroyed," when the people of Nineveh*
> *believed God; they proclaimed a fast and all*
> *of them, great and small, put on sackcloth.*
> *(Jonah 3:4ff)*

The Hebrew text reads: "Forty days more and
Nineveh shall be destroyed." But the ancient Greek
Septuagint translation, probably reading a different
Hebrew manuscript, translates: "Three days
more...." The three days is most likely the right
reading since it harmonizes much better with the
fast action of the rest of the story. Why should the
author have Jonah rush down to the boat, move in
and out of the whale so quickly and then straight
over to Nineveh only to slow everything down with
a forty-day wait? The fast action is one of the
book's most attractive features. It gives us a bird's-
eye view of man that we don't find in the great and
more verbose prophets. Those Assyrians, after all,
didn't need forty days to make up their minds to
repent. Perhaps the forty-day reading was slipped

in by someone like us who needs it.

The Jews in Jonah's day had a very high opinion of themselves and a very low one of everybody else. They felt that they really deserved God's love, while the pagans had earned severe chastisement. Thus during the Babylonian exile, when they saw what hard times they had fallen into and how well life was going for their pagan captors, they cried:

> It is vain to serve God, and what do we profit by keeping his command, and going about in penitential dress in awe of the Lord of hosts? Rather we must call the proud blessed; for indeed evildoers prosper, and even tempt God with impunity. (Malachi 3:14ff)

This attitude is very similar to that of the elder son in the parable of the Prodigal Son:

> For years now I have slaved for you. I never disobeyed one of your orders, yet you never gave me so much as a kid goat to celebrate with my friends. Then, when this son of yours returns after having gone through your property with loose women, you kill the fatted calf for him. (Luke 15:29ff)

But God pardoned both Nineveh and the younger son because they were converted from their evil ways. Their humility had saved them and prepared them for conversion. But the self-satisfied attitude of the self-styled just shuts out any hope of their conversion. They feel no need for a justification freely granted by God. Their own false righteousness is all they want.

When the king of Nineveh got up and called for conversion, he was expressing hope that God would pardon them. Every converted sinner is a witness to hope. Today this witness is one of the Christian's essential duties. The Old Testament had already seen that man is a being who hopes, who awaits the future with expectancy. However, it saw the futility of placing one's hope in man and of human hope in general which may or may not be fulfilled. God alone is man's hope. Israel is built on God's promises to the patriarchs and on faith in his fidelity to those promises. Hope is therefore no secondary idea in the Old Testament, but woven into the most essential fabric of man's relation with God. It implies three elements: a future expectation, confidence in awaiting its coming and patience to bear the difficulties in the meantime. The king and his people showed that they had all three and God did not disappoint their hope.

In Jonah's message to Nineveh there was not a word about conversion. He simply announced that the city would be destroyed. The Ninevites suggested and carried out the conversion themselves. What a contrast these Assyrians present to the Jews, who had received and rejected constant and explicit conversion calls from a whole series of prophets. This was one of the author's intentions: to awaken his contemporaries to an inner personal conversion through the comparison he so subtly suggests.

The king of Nineveh admonished his people: " . . . every man shall turn from his evil way and from the violence he has in hand." *(Jonah 3:8)* The Assyrians were one of the most violent nations in history. The prophet Nahum stressed their violence in his oracle on the fall of Nineveh: "Woe to the bloody city, all lies, full of plunder, whose looting never stops!" *(Nahum 3:1)* The Bible views the shedding of human blood as a special sin against "God's image." The Hebrew word for blood, *dam*, came to be an ethical-juridical term to designate homicide. Thus Hosea describes Samaria as a city where "blood touches blood," i.e. where murder follows murder *(Hosea 4:2)*. Murder is the worst form of man's domination over other men. When God created man as his own image, he willed that he dominate the earth, but not that he be dominated by other men. One man's domination of another is not God's intention and leads to man's perdition. As Ecclesiastes remarks: " . . . I applied my mind to every work that is done under the sun, while one man tyrannizes over another to his hurt." *(Ecclesiastes 8:9)*

Some of the prophecies such as Isaiah 2:2-4 foresee a universal peace in which: "They [the nations] shall beat their swords into plowshares and their spears into pruning hooks." Instruments of death will be replaced by those of life. However, this peace is regarded as a gift from the "God of peace" *(Romans 15:33)* and not something which can be conquered by human means alone. The ancient Israelites were not tempted, as we are today, to make hope itself a god. They did not believe that they could build the new heaven and earth by their own forces. The modern attempt to do so can only end by making the present world uninhabitable. The Christian today must let the world know that the only thing that can save it from its own self-destruction is conversion. Nineveh was saved by sackcloth and ashes, not by battle dress and bombs.

It is tempting to speculate about just what effect a really converted Nineveh would have had on the history of the ancient Near East and on the world. If there really had been a Jonah who had managed to convert that powerful and bloodthirsty nation, not to Yahweh, but just to morally good conduct, what a tremendous influence for good it might have been. If Asurbanipal or Tiglath-pileser III had really undergone a conversion, the whole course of history might have been as different as if Cleopatra's nose had been longer.

The Christian receives a new self-understanding through baptism and the conversion which precedes it. He sees his relation to God, to other men and to himself in a new light. This will necessarily create a tension in his life and demand many renunciations in order to live according to his new world-picture and defend it against the attacks of his lower instincts, which want to obscure and control it. But just as man's reason should control and regulate his animal nature, so the new spiritual light the Christian has received should rule over his human nature without destroying it, but rather developing it. When Jonah's message sounded in the streets of Nineveh, the Ninevites acquired a new self-understanding. But they realized that without exercising it, without expressing and controlling it through fasting and sackcloth, they would not keep it alive.

The Ninevites, who were so famous for their violence, realized that this violence would have to go and explicitly state in their conversion program that every man must turn "from the violence he has in hand." However, Jesus spoke of a new kind of violence, without which no one will enter his kingdom *(Matthew 11:12)*. This violence includes the will and perseverance necessary for a real conversion. The Ninevites proved that they had it.

If Nineveh's conversion was sincere, as we know it was, the Ninevites had to continue their ascetical life after the city was spared. They certainly couldn't go about their daily lives, however, clothed in sackcloth. But they found the necessary asceticism built into the activities and sufferings of their everyday existence. Their heavy and humiliating forms of work, their lack of technology and many other aspects of life in that period all carried a good dose of asceticism with them. Although we have a technology that they didn't enjoy, our greater nervousness perhaps makes ordinary existence more of a penitential exercise than it was in those hardy days. The tension produced by a greatly increased world population with all the problems of conviviality it implies can also provide us with a very viable source of renunciation.

Whatever forms of mortification the Ninevites went in for after their conversion, they only did their job if they were subordinated to the theological life of faith, hope and charity. These three virtues and attitudes structure man's relation with God under both the Old and New Alliances. Asceticism is a means of furthering their growth. One of the causes behind Jonah's lack of the spirit of faith, which his flight implied, may well have been his failure to mortify his intellect so that faith could develop there. He allowed his mind to be clouded by his passionate nationalism and his hatred of foreign countries. This kept the doctrine of Hosea and Jeremiah on the primacy of an interior conversion and communion with God over all exterior religious relations, from sinking in and blinded him to the solid lesson in Second Isaiah on God's preoccupation for all nations. Modern communication media today assault the intellect on all sides. Every Christian must develop some sort of intellectual armor to protect his mind from exposure to these instruments. Otherwise his intellect will not remain free. The passions aroused by the news media also make universal love very difficult. They incite one to hatred, vengeance and a desire to dominate other nations much more than to mutual love and understanding. They thus attack the Christian's charity as well as his faith. They likewise arouse his sexual desires and his craving for more material goods. They lead him to fix his hope on material things and thereby weaken theological hope. Hence no Christian today can expect to lead a deep theological life without accepting many renunciations.

Many Christians looked for some sort of mass miracle, such as that which followed on Jonah's preaching, to take place after Vatican II. The high theological tone of the conciliar texts, as well as the plain common sense in many of them, aroused great enthusiasm in many quarters. When the anticipated collective conversion didn't take place, a wave of discouragement swept over many people. They felt like Jonah when the worm got his gourd. They had overlooked the resistance to grace that can exist in men and in institutions, and the vital part that human liberty plays in every conversion. The modern Ninevites heard the conciliar words and went right on with their old ways. They even felt stimulated to harden their own positions and attitudes. But a Jonah attitude is certainly not Christian. No one knew better than St. Paul the bitterness that obstinate human opposition can bring into the life of someone who is trying to build up the Church. Yet his problems with the Judaizers and the pagan authorities did not keep him from becoming the theologian of Christian joy. He knew that joy in tribulation is always possible for the Christian, since this joy is a fruit of the Holy Spirit and does not depend on the condition of our gastric juices when we wake up in the morning.

One reason why so many felt dismayed after Vatican II is that they had lived like children under the collective shadow of a Church united by the doctrinal and disciplinary coherence which has characterized it since the Council of Trent. They had grown accustomed to the protection and sense of security which this gave. They felt as cooled and comforted by the Church's monolithic structure, and by the firm and paternal leadership of a series of great popes, as Jonah did beneath his gourd. But Vatican II proved to be the worm in the gourd and many of us are reacting like Jonah. We are now asked to be creative rather than conformative, to incite to new life and light new fires rather than live like parasites on the inheritance of our fathers in the faith and warm ourselves in the glow of centuries-old flames. God is calling us to say good-bye to the gourd without regret and to learn to live in the sunlight and freedom of mature Christians.

The Mystery of Mercy

"I beseech you, Lord," he prayed, *"is not this what I said while I was still in my own country? This is why I fled at first to Tarshish. I knew that you are a gracious and merciful God, slow to anger, rich in clemency, loathe to punish!" (Jonah 4:2)*

One of the chief lessons in Jonah is that the relation between God and man is characterized by merciful love on God's part and by faith on man's. The book's author thus not only overturns the views of his hero, Jonah the nationalistic Jew, but those of the entire pagan world as well. For in Greek literature the God-man relation is governed by envy and fear on the gods' side, who see man as a rival and so fear his assaults on them and envy his happiness, while on man's side hubris, or arrogant pride and rebellion, mark his conduct. Thus when Prometheus is chained to a rock on the mountain, he says he would prefer to stay that way rather than humble himself by begging mercy from the gods.

The gospel parable of the workers in the vineyard *(Matthew 20:1-16)* has some likeness to the message of the book of Jonah. In strict justice, those who only put in an hour on the job had no right to receive the same wage as those who worked all day. They earned an hour's pay for an hour's work. But the master of the yard decides to be generous and, out of sheer goodness, pays them a day's wage for an hour's work. Instead of admiring and praising the master's goodness, the other workers are envious and critical. They are like the Pharisees who murmur about Jesus' conduct with sinners. Jonah had no doubt been a good man or God would not have called him to a prophetic mission and kept him going when he backed out. But Jonah just hated to see people he thought worthy of instant death having a share in the same mercy he lived on. He was thus one of the first critics of divine love and mercy. His eye was evil because God was good.

The First book of Kings shows us, in chapter 19, how Elijah fled a day's journey into the desert during his flight from Jezebel, sat down exhausted under a broom tree and said: "This is enough, O Lord! Take my life, for I am no better than my fathers." *(1 Kings 19:4)* Like Jonah, he was worn out. Like Jonah, too, he sat down in the shade. And like Jonah again, he uses the formula: "Lord, take my life." The scholars speak of a dependence of the author of Jonah on this passage from Kings. But there is also room for a comparison between the two prophets. Elijah, who cut down 450 prophets of Baal in the brook Kishon and insisted that none be allowed to escape, who called down fire on two detachments of soldiers, had no doubt passed on some of his prophetic zeal to Jonah. But both of them had to learn about mercy from God. Elijah got his lesson in the cave on Horeb when God told him he was not in the wind, the earthquake or the fire, but in "a tiny whispering sound." *(1 Kings 19:12)* Jonah's lesson came after the worm got his gourd. Each of us has to learn the same thing.

The author of Jonah has a modern spiritual daughter in St. Thérèse of Lisieux. She tells us that she saw all God's attributes through his mercy, even his justice. For her God's justice was the quality by which he took our human weakness into account. She would find mercy not only for the Assyrians and the prodigal son, but even for Jonah, for the prodigal's elder brother and for herself: "Ah! must not the infinitely just God, who deigns to pardon the faults of the prodigal son with so much kindness, be just also towards me who 'am always with him?'" She tells us too that God's justice is the foundation for her joy and trust. "To be just means not only to exercise severity in punishing the guilty, but also to recognize right intentions and reward virtue. I hope as much from the good God's justice as from his mercy — because He 'is compassionate and merciful, long-suffering and plentious in mercy.'" The last quotation from Psalm 103 is the same formula invoked by Jonah when he saw that, much to his disgust, God had pardoned Nineveh: "I knew that you are a gracious and merciful God, slow to anger, rich in clemency, loath to punish." *(Jonah 4:2)* But we must not be too hard on our hero; he had his faults like all of us, and we can hope that he went back to Palestine a new man and ready to spread the message of mercy and love.

St. Thérèse of Lisieux had an attraction for Assyrians and prodigal sons rather than an aversion. As a child she had prayed and sacrificed for the conversion of a notorious killer named Pranzini. She also had a special love for St. Augustine and St. Mary Magdalene. She says of the latter: "I feel that her heart realized the fathomless depths of love and mercy in Jesus' Heart, realized, despite her sins, that that Heart was ready not only to pardon her but actually to lavish on her the treasures of his divine intimacy and raise her to the highest summits of contemplation." And she says elsewhere: "Even though I had on my conscience all the sins that can be committed, I would go, my heart broken with sorrow, and throw myself into Jesus' arms, for I know how much he loves the prodigal child who returns to him." Thérèse would find Jonah's attitude hard to understand, but she would certainly find a kindred spirit in the book's author.

The message of the book of Jonah, like that of the gospel parables, is hard for most of us to accept. For we find it hard to believe that God is grace, that he loves, that he is sheer goodness. We shy away from a God who is all these and who offers us too our liberty with which we can respond to him without, however, being able to manipulate him. The book of Jonah and the parables show us God seeking man, preoccupied for man, hoping for his return, inviting and encouraging him, overlooking his smallness and narrowness and remaining his father no matter how great his sins are. Most of the parables have the wrong names in our editions of the New Testament. Their main actor is not man, but God. The central figure in the story of the prodigal son, for example, is not the lost boy but the loving and patient father, who will defend his son against his elder brother when he returns. God thus proves that he is a better friend to man than man is either to himself or to his fellowman. This is very clear in Jonah. God defends the Assyrians against Jonah and the Jews. God is solicitous about them and this lesson, which is applied to the Assyrians in Jonah, will be referred to every man in the parables.

Jonah really hated the Assyrians. This shouldn't surprise us because it was the common feeling among the Israelites of his day. God only taught men very gradually how to love their enemies and to do good to those who hate them. We can see the universal problem raised by human conviviality represented in the little story of Cain and Abel in Genesis. The key word "brother" comes up seven times in the narrative. Two brothers living in different social structures — one a farmer, the other a herdsman — clash and the one who feels slighted kills the other and then refuses all responsibility for him *(Genesis 4:9)*. Modern society is still struggling with the same problem.

Two Old Testament texts show real progress in Israel's assimilation of God's message of fraternal love. In Exodus 23:4ff, the law of Deuteronomy directs that if the Israelite came upon his enemy's lost ox or ass, he should give it back to him. And if he finds his enemy's ass falling under its load, he should help it. This taught Israel that the animal's need was to be placed before his own hatred for his enemy. Another text shows that the enemy's needs are to be preferred to the Israelite's hatred for him:

If your enemy be hungry, give him food to eat, if he be thirsty, give him to drink;
For live coals you will heap on his head, and the Lord will vindicate you. (Proverbs 25:21ff)

Egyptian texts from this period show that in Egyptian penitential rites live coals were put on the repentant person's head as a sign of his shame and repentance for his faults. The Israelite, therefore, may hope that by helping an enemy in need he will cause him to feel ashamed of himself and seek reconciliation. The book of Jonah makes an important contribution to the doctrine of fraternal charity by manifesting God's great love for Israel's most hated enemy. It implicitly invites the Jews and all of us to love as God does.

Certainly in our era of hot and cold wars, of détente and confrontation, the book of Jonah's attack on exaggerated nationalism is tremendously important. It is not easy to love those who form a different nation and who have inflicted injuries on us while proclaiming their hatred for us and for all we represent. It took centuries for the Jews to even accept the idea and much less to practice it. The prophet Amos broke ground for this lesson in the eighth century. He told his contemporaries that God not only brought them out of Egypt, but that he had led the other nations as well into their present territories *(Amos 9:7).* So God was concerned about the other nations. The author of the second part of Isaiah, who lived in Babylon during the Israelite captivity there, saw how silly it was to treat the pagans like horned monsters without knowing them. He therefore depicted the Servant of the Lord as arising from Israel and dying for the pagans in order to form "a covenant of the people" from all nations *(Isaiah 42:1-4, 6-7, etc.).* The same idea is developed in some other late parts of Isaiah. Chapter 19:23-25 shows Egypt and Assyria sharing in God's blessing. And chapter 25:6-8, one of the tenderest pictures of God in the Bible and one of the strongest defenses of universalism, describes all nations united in a great feast when death is destroyed and God wipes the tears from everyone's eyes. For the Jews this meant that God's hand would be bent lovingly over the Assyrians, and for us today it means that the same divine hand will touch the Russians, North Koreans, etc.

If Amos insisted on the equality of all nations before God's justice, the book of Jonah moves the accent to God's love. God loves Jonah. This is clear from the care with which he prepares a special whale to swallow him and a private gourd to shade him. But God loves the Assyrians too. He has cultivated them with all the care a good gardener lavishes on his plants. This was, of course, a revolutionary doctrine at that time. It was startling for the Jews to see the formula "Yahweh, a merciful and gracious God, slow to anger and rich in kindness and fidelity," which originally referred to Israel's own relation with God *(Exodus 34:6)*, now being applied to God's care for the Assyrians. The book of Ruth had shown them that a foreigner, a Moabite, could be an exemplary woman and become incorporated into Israel, but this only meant that there was a chance for pagans to become naturalized Jews. Jonah goes further. The author shows that an Assyrian can remain an Assyrian and still be loved by God provided that he be a morally good Assyrian. We can see that even in St. Paul's day the Jews had not yet overcome their prejudice against foreigners. For when he told the Jerusalem Jews that God was sending him to the pagans, they shouted and threw dust into the air (*Acts 22:22-23*).

The book of Jonah deserves a place of honor in every Christian heart. It picks up the purest current of prophetic tradition on God's love and goodness and man's need to return that love. It applies some of the most profound lessons in Hosea and Jeremiah on the heart of God with gentle humor and in few words. It is not surprising then to find that Jesus developed its teaching in his parable of the prodigal son. Here we find a contrast between the father's attitude toward the sinful boy and that of the elder son which is very similar to that between God's generous conduct with the Assyrians and Jonah's resentment of such behavior. Both stories have the same literary structure and message. The prodigal sins and Nineveh sins, yet God continues to love both. The son keeps on being a beloved son and Nineveh a beloved city. The son repents and so does Nineveh. In both cases the pardon is loving and full and accompanied with great joy. If Jonah loves his gourd and rejoices over it, God's love and joy over Nineveh are greater still. In both stories God's conduct provokes a satirical criticism of this narrow and hateful attitude. But, in both cases, God is very gentle in his admonition of the egoist: "My son . . . you are with me always, and everything I have is yours . . . " *(Luke 15:31ff)*, and Jonah receives the book's tender closing words.

The parable of the prodigal son was originally spoken by Jesus to condemn the Pharisees for excluding sinners from God's kingdom. One result of their religious snobbery was that they shut themselves out from that kingdom. Jesus makes this clear in several places *(Luke 18:14*, for example). So when Jesus first told the story, the elder son was a symbol of the Pharisees. However, later on St. Luke wanted to use the story in the early Church to teach something to his fellow Christians rather than to the Pharisees. He therefore modified the parable and made the elder son also an object of the father's love, and by no means excluded from the kingdom, and thus able to represent those Christians who still found it hard to understand God's mercy toward their sinful fellow Christians. So the message of Jonah was applied to the Pharisees by Jesus and to the early Christians by St. Luke. The book has then a real Christian dimension.

The book of Jonah's climax is, of course, God's closing words to his depressed prophet — You feel compassion for a gourd that didn't cost you any effort and shouldn't I have compassion on all these men and cattle whom I created and love? If you feel sorry for a gourd you didn't plant shouldn't I feel sorry for and pardon these men whom I created in my image? If the death of this little tree can cause you so much pain, how do you think I feel about the death of one hundred and twenty thousand men and all their cattle, to say nothing of this huge city? — It would be hard to find a better description of the heart of God where mercy and compassion win out over justice. Yet his justice is not omitted. He was prepared to destroy the city but, since they have sincerely repented, he now gives free rein to his mercy. Jeremiah had already spoken an oracle in this same line:

Sometimes I threaten to uproot and tear down and destroy a nation or a kingdom. But if that nation which I have threatened turns from its evil, I also repent of the evil which I threatened to do. (Jeremiah 18:7ff)

Even though God gave Jonah a gourd for shade, verse five of chapter four has him dwelling in a hut. But this hut shouldn't be there. Verse five has all the characteristics of a later insertion. It doesn't agree with what came before, for Jonah no longer had any hope that God would spare the city and couldn't be waiting to see what would happen. God had already pardoned the city and Jonah had already complained about it. But verse five also disagrees with what follows it, for verse eight shows that Jonah had no other protection from the sun except his gourd-tree. If he had been living in a hut, God would not have needed to provide him with a shade tree. There is good reason for the gourd being in the book, because God leads Jonah out of Nineveh to give him a lesson by means of the gourd. But there is no reason for the hut being

there except some later copyist's feeling that if
Jonah was going to have a forty-day wait on his
hands, he would need some sort of shelter. But the
original text seems to have read three and not forty
days, as the Septuagint shows. We see Israel's living
tradition at work here not only preserving the text,
but also trying to clarify it and make it more
understandable. If Jonah was going to be there for
forty days, he at least would not have to-sleep in
the rain.

Even in the Old Testament it is obvious that
God destined man to love and not to hate. A beautiful sentence in Micah sums up man's conduct:

> *You have been told, O man, what is good
> and what the Lord requires of you: Only to
> do the right and to love goodness, and to walk
> humbly with your God. (Micah 6:8)*

This love should not only include fellow Israelites, but all men. This is brought out in the prophetic passages about the universality of God's
kingdom as well as in the blessing of the patriarchs.
Thus in Genesis 12:3, Abraham's blessing is to
extend to the whole world. And in Isaiah 19:24ff,
Israel is presented as a blessing for her enemies:

> *On that day Israel shall be a third party
> with Egypt and Assyria, a blessing in the
> midst of the land, when the Lord of hosts
> blesses it: "Blessed be my people Egypt, and
> the work of my hands Assyria, and my inheri-
> tance, Israel."*

These texts would have been hard for Jonah to
bear, yet St. Paul picks up the same thought by
telling us that through Jesus Abraham's blessing
will reach all men *(Galatians 3:8)*.

Throughout the whole story God's action on Jonah is directed to developing the theological life of faith, hope and love in the prophet. These are the three powers by which God's life grows in us, by which we Christians call him "father" and are guided by the Holy Spirit in our following of Christ. Even though Jonah lived under the ancient covenant and never knew Christ, the structure of his spiritual life is the same as ours. He was preparing the world for Christ's coming; we are living in the full light of that event. But for him, as for us, Christ is the center of existence: implicitly in his case, explicitly in ours. Jonah shows us how hard it is for the theological life to develop in man. He indicates by his flight just how weak his faith was. Through his discouragement after Nineveh's conversion, we can see how feeble hope was in his life. And in his hatred of the Assyrians, we have a picture of very poorly rooted love. However, we must not judge Jonah in the light of a gospel he never heard, but according to the stage of revelation in which he lived. Seen in this light, he was pretty good, he was learning to love.

There are saints, like St. John of the Cross, who never made a major mistake. It is, therefore, hard for us to identify with them. But the author of the book of Jonah presented us with a different kind of hero. His biography opened with a huge blunder and closed with him flat on his back wishing he were dead. Even though he passed through an intense purification in the whale's belly, he was still not up to treading the lofty path of heroic virtue. He still couldn't take those Assyrians and was very attached to his gourd. Jonah was a man who really needed the simple evangelical doctrine that St. Thérèse of Lisieux would perfect centuries later showing us how to capitalize on our weakness and blunders and approach God on his weak side:

his infinite merciful love, which can't refuse anyone who comes with humility and loving trust.

One thing the book of Jonah and Vatican II have in common is their universal vision. They are both against selectivities and segregations, separated minorities and zealots, i.e. those groups or persons who place their own national or ideological collectivity before the totality of men. When the author of Jonah condemns and satirizes our hero for being narrowly nationalistic, and when he shows how much God loves the Assyrians, he was fighting for the same cause as Vatican II when it called the Church the people of God. The Council's intention was not so much a contrast with the former hierarchical vision of the Church, but rather an emphasis on the Church as a people called together by God's word from all nations and regions of the earth. It will always be necessary to have small groups formed and working in the Church, but these must never exist solely or primarily to cultivate themselves, but to serve the totality. All small groups are called to act as a ferment for the whole and not as a cancer living at the body's expense.

Both the book of Jonah and St. Matthew's Gospel close with God asking men to be more spiritually broadminded, to extend their love in ever greater circles. Jonah is urged to love the Assyrians and Jesus tells his apostles:

> ". . . go, therefore, and make disciples of all the nations. Baptize them in the name of the Father, and of the Son, and of the Holy Spirit. Teach them to carry out everything I have commanded you. And know that I am with you always, until the end of the world!" (Matthew 28:19ff)

So the Church exists to keep alive Christ's memory among men, to preserve his words living in their memories, to make him known and loved by them, and to arouse in them a hope for his return in the parousia. God is calling every Christian today to participate in this mission, to carry the message of his mercy, now incarnate in Christ, to the modern Nineveh, to help create eternal life for men who still cannot distinguish their right hand from their left. If we accept his invitation, we ourselves will be the first to enjoy that life.

The Book of Jonah

CHAPTER 1

The First Mission. ¹ This is the word of the Lord
that came to Jonah, son of Amittai: ² "Set out for
the great city of Nineveh, and preach against it;
their wickedness has come up before me." ³ But
Jonah made ready to flee to Tarshish away from
the Lord. He went down to Joppa, found a ship
going to Tarshish, paid the fare, and went aboard
to journey with them to Tarshish, away from the
Lord.

⁴ The Lord, however, hurled a violent wind upon
the sea, and in the furious tempest that arose the
ship was on the point of breaking up. ⁵ Then the
mariners became frightened and each one cried to
his god. To lighten the ship for themselves, they
threw its cargo into the sea. Meanwhile, Jonah had
gone down into the hold of the ship, and lay there
fast asleep. ⁶ The captain came to him and said,
"What are you doing asleep? Rise up, call upon
your God! Perhaps God will be mindful of us so
that we may not perish."

⁷ Then they said to one another, "Come, let us
cast lots to find out on whose account we have met

with this misfortune." So they cast lots, and thus singled out Jonah. ⁸ "Tell us," they said, "what is your business? Where do you come from? What is your country, and to what people do you belong?" ⁹ "I am a Hebrew," Jonah answered them; "I worship the Lord, the God of heaven, who made the sea and the dry land."

¹⁰ Now the men were seized with great fear and said to him, "How could you do such a thing!" — They knew that he was fleeing from the Lord, because he had told them. — ¹¹ "What shall we do with you," they asked, "that the sea may quiet down for us?" For the sea was growing more and more turbulent. ¹² Jonah said to them, "Pick me up and throw me into the sea, that it may quiet down for you; since I know it is because of me that this violent storm has come upon you."

¹³ Still the men rowed hard to regain the land, but they could not, for the sea grew ever more turbulent. ¹⁴ Then they cried to the Lord: "We beseech you, O Lord, let us not perish for taking this man's life; do not charge us with shedding innocent blood, for you, Lord, have done as you saw fit." ¹⁵ Then they took Jonah and threw him into the sea, and the sea's raging abated. ¹⁶ Struck with great fear of the Lord, the men offered sacrifice and made vows to him.

CHAPTER 2

¹ But the Lord sent a large fish, that swallowed Jonah; and he remained in the belly of the fish three days and three nights. ² From the belly of the fish Jonah said this prayer to the Lord, his God:

³ Out of my distress I called to the Lord, and he
   answered me;
  From the midst of the nether world I cried for
   help,
   and you heard my voice.
⁴ For you cast me into the deep, into the heart of
   the sea,
   and the flood enveloped me;
  All your breakers and your billows passed over
   me.
⁵ Then I said, "I am banished from your sight!
   yet would I again look upon your holy temple."
⁶ The waters swirled about me, threatening my
   life;
   the abyss enveloped me;
   seaweed clung about my head.
⁷ Down I went to the roots of the mountains;
   the bars of the nether world
   were closing behind me forever,
  But you brought up my life from the pit,
   O Lord, my God.

⁸ When my soul fainted within me, I remembered
   the Lord;
  My prayer reached you in your holy temple.
⁹ Those who worship vain idols forsake their
   source of mercy.
¹⁰ But I, with resounding praise, will sacrifice to
   you;
  What I have vowed I will pay: deliverance is
   from the Lord.
¹¹ Then the Lord commanded the fish to spew
   Jonah upon the shore.

CHAPTER 3

Conversion of Nineveh. ¹ The word of the Lord came to Jonah a second time: ² "Set out for the great city of Nineveh, and announce to it the message that I will tell you." ³ So Jonah made ready and went to Nineveh, according to the Lord's bidding. Now Nineveh was an enormously large city; it took three days to go through it. ⁴ Jonah began his journey through the city, and had gone but a single day's walk announcing, "Forty days more and Nineveh shall be destroyed," ⁵ when the people of Nineveh believed God; they proclaimed a fast and all of them, great and small, put on sackcloth.

⁶ When the news reached the king of Nineveh, he rose from his throne, laid aside his robe, covered himself with sackcloth, and sat in the ashes. ⁷ Then he had this proclaimed throughout Nineveh, by decree of the king and his nobles: "Neither man nor beast, neither cattle nor sheep, shall taste anything; they shall not eat, nor shall they drink water. ⁸ Man and beast shall be covered with sackcloth and call loudly to God; every man shall turn from his evil way and from the violence he has in hand. ⁹ Who knows, God may relent and forgive, and withhold his blazing wrath, so that we shall not perish." ¹⁰ When God saw by their actions how they turned from their evil way, he repented of the evil that he had threatened to do to them; he did not carry it out.

CHAPTER 4

Jonah's Anger: God's Reproof. ¹ But this was greatly displeasing to Jonah, and he became angry. ² "I beseech you, Lord," he prayed, "is not this what I said while I was still in my own country? This is why I fled at first to Tarshish. I knew that you are a gracious and merciful God, slow to anger, rich in clemency, loathe to punish. ³ And now, Lord, please take my life from me; for it is better for me to die than to live." ⁴ But the Lord asked, "Have you reason to be angry?"

⁵ Jonah then left the city for a place to the east of it, where he built himself a hut and waited under it in the shade, to see what would happen to the city. ⁶ And when the Lord God provided a gourd plant, that grew up over Jonah's head, giving shade that relieved him of any discomfort, Jonah was very happy over the plant. ⁷ But the next morning at dawn God sent a worm which attacked the plant, so that it withered. ⁸ And when the sun arose, God sent a burning east wind; and the sun beat upon Jonah's head till he became faint. Then he asked for death, saying, "I would be better off dead than alive."

⁹ But God said to Jonah, "Have you reason to be angry over the plant?" "I have reason to be angry," Jonah answered, "angry enough to die." ¹⁰ Then the Lord said, "You are concerned over the plant which cost you no labor and which you did not raise; it came up in one night and in one night it perished. ¹¹ And should I not be concerned over Nineveh, the great city, in which there are more than a hundred and twenty thousand persons who cannot distinguish their right hand from their left, not to mention the many cattle?"

JONAH:
Spirituality of a Runaway Prophet
1.75

Roman Ginn, o.c.s.o. While acquiring a new appreciation for this very human prophet, we come to see that his story is really our own. It reveals a God whose love is unwavering yet demanding, for if we are to experience the freedom of mature Christians, we must enter the darkness of the tomb with Christ, as Jonah did, in order to rise to new life.

POOR IN SPIRIT:
Awaiting All From God
1.75

Cardinal Garrone. Not a biography of the Mother Teresa of her age, this spiritual account of Jeanne Jugan's complete and joyful abandonment to God leads us to a vibrant understanding of spiritual and material poverty. This founder of the Little Sisters of the Poor left behind a life that is a spiritual classic, inspiring us in our search to live as the Lord would have us.

... AND I WILL FILL THIS HOUSE WITH GLORY:
Renewal Within a Suburban Parish
1.50

Rev. James A. Brassil. This book helps answer the questions: What is the Charismatic Renewal doing for the Church as a whole? and What is the prayer group doing for the parish? With a vibrant prayer life and a profound devotion to the Eucharist, this Long Island prayer group has successfully endured the growing pains inherent to the spiritual life, the fruit of which is offered to the reader.

DESERT SILENCE:
A Way of Prayer for an Unquiet Age
1.75

Rev. Alan J. Placa. The pioneering efforts of the men and women of the early church who went out into the desert to find union with the Lord has relevance for those of us today who are seeking the pure uncluttered desert place within to have it filled with the loving silence of God's presence.

Order from your bookstore or
LIVING FLAME PRESS, Locust Valley, N.Y. 11560

PRAYING WITH SCRIPTURE IN THE HOLY LAND:
Daily Meditations With the Risen Jesus
2.25

Msgr. David E. Rosage. Herein is offered a daily meeting with the Risen Jesus in those Holy Places which He sanctified by His human presence. Three hundred and sixty-five scripture texts are selected and blended with the pilgrimage experiences of the author, a retreat master, and well-known writer on prayer.

DISCOVERING PATHWAYS TO PRAYER
1.75

Msgr. David E. Rosage. Following Jesus was never meant to be dull, or worse, just duty-filled. Those who would aspire to a life of prayer and those who have already begun, will find this book amazingly thorough in its scripture-punctuated approach.

"A simple but profound book which explains the many ways and forms of prayer by which the person hungering for closer union with God may find him." **Emmnauel Spillane, O.C.S.O., Abbot, Our Lady of the Holy Trinity Abbey, Huntsville, Utah.**

REASONS FOR REJOICING
Experiences in Christian Hope
1.75

Rev. Kenneth J. Zanca. The author asks: "Do we really or rarely have a sense of excitement, mystery, and wonder in the presence of God?" His book offers a path to rejuvenation in Christian faith, hope, and love. It deals with prayer, forgiveness, worship and other religious experiences in a learned and penetrating, yet simple, non-technical manner. **Religion Teachers' Journal.**

"It is a refreshing Christian approach to the Good News, always emphasizing the love and mercy of God in our lives, and our response to that love in Christian hope." **Brother Patrick Hart, Secretary to the late Thomas Merton.**

CONTEMPLATIVE PRAYER:
Problems and An Approach for the Ordinary Christian
1.75

Rev. Alan J. Placa. This inspiring book covers much ground: the struggle of prayer, growth in familiarity with the Lord and the sharing process. In addition, he clearly outlines a method of contemplative prayer for small groups based on the belief that private communion with God is essential to, and must precede, shared prayer. The last chapter provides model prayers, taken from our Western heritage, for the enrichment of private prayer experience.

THE ONE WHO LISTENS:
A Book of Prayer   2.25

Rev. Michael Hollings and Etta Gullick. Here the Spirit speaks through men and women of the past (St. John of the Cross, Thomas More, Dietrich Bonhoeffer), and present (Michel Quoist, Mother Teresa, Malcolm Boyd). There are also prayers from men of other faiths such as Muhammed and Tagore. God meets us where we are and since men share in sorrow, joy and anxiety, *their* prayers are *our* prayers. This is a book that will be outworn, perhaps, but never outgrown.

ENFOLDED BY CHRIST:
An Encouragement to Pray   1.95

Rev. Michael Hollings. This book helps us toward giving our lives to God in prayer yet at the same time remaining totally available to our fellowman — a difficult but possible feat. Father's sharing of his own difficulties and his personal approach convince us that "if he can do it, we can." We find in the author a true spiritual guardian and friend.

PETALS OF PRAYER:
Creative Ways to Pray   1.50

Rev. Paul Sauvé. *"Petals of Prayer is an extremely practical book for anyone who desires to pray but has difficulty finding a method for so doing. At least 15 different methods of prayer are described and illustrated in simple, straightforward ways, showing they can be contemporary even though many of them enjoy a tradition of hundreds of years. In an excellent introductory chapter, Fr. Sauvé states that the best 'method' of prayer is the one which unites us to God. . . . Father Sauvé masterfully shows how traditional methods of prayer can be very much in tune with a renewed church."* **St. Anthony Messenger.**

Order from your bookstore or
LIVING FLAME PRESS, Locust Valley, N.Y. 11560

CRISIS OF FAITH:
Invitation to Christian Maturity
1.50

Rev. Thomas Keating, o.c.s.o. How to hear ourselves called to discipleship in the Gospels is Abbot Thomas' important and engrossing message. As Our Lord forms His disciples, and deals with His friends or with those who come asking for help in the Gospels, we can receive insights into the way He is forming or dealing with us in our day to day lives.

IN GOD'S PROVIDENCE:
The Birth of a Catholic Charismatic Parish
1.50

Rev. John Randall. The engrossing story of the now well-known Word of God Prayer Community in St. Patrick's Parish, Providence, Rhode Island, as it developed from Father Randall's first adverse reaction to the budding Charismatic Movement to today as it copes with the problems of being a truly pioneer Catholic Charismatic Parish.

"This splendid little volume bubbles over with joy and peace, with 'Spirit' and work." **The Priest.**

SOURCE OF LIFE:
The Eucharist and Christian Living
1.50

Rev. Rene Voillaume. A powerful testimony to the vital part the Eucharist plays in the life of a Christian. It is a product of a man for whom Christ in the Eucharist is nothing less than all.

SEEKING PURITY OF HEART:
The Gift of Ourselves to God
illus. 1.25

Joseph Breault. For those of us who feel that we do not live up to God's calling, that we have sin of whatever shade within our hearts. This book shows how we can begin a journey which will lead from our personal darkness to wholeness in Christ's light — a purity of heart. Clear, practical help is given us in the constant struggle to free ourselves from the deceptions that sin has planted along all avenues of our lives.

PROMPTED BY THE SPIRIT 2.25

Rev. Paul Sauvé. A handbook by a Catholic Charismatic Renewal national leader for all seriously concerned about the future of the renewal and interested in finding answers to some of the problems that have surfaced in small or large prayer groups. It is a call to all Christians to find answers with the help of a wise Church tradition as transmitted by her ordained ministers. The author has also written *Petals of Prayer/Creative Ways to Pray.*

DISCOVERING PATHWAYS TO PRAYER 1.75

Msgr. David E. Rosage. Following Jesus was never meant to be dull, or worse, just duty-filled. Those who would aspire to a life of prayer and those who have already begun, will find this book amazingly thorough in its scripture-punctuated approach.

"A simple but profound book which explains the many ways and forms of prayer by which the person hungering for closer union with God may find him." **Emmanuel Spillane, O.C.S.O., Abbot, Our Lady of the Holy Trinity Abbey, Huntsville, Utah.**

THE BOOK OF REVELATION:
What Does It Really Say? 1.75

Rev. John Randall, S.T.D. The most discussed book of the Bible today is examined by a scripture expert in relation to much that has been published on the Truth. A simply written and revealing presentation.

Order from your bookstore or
LIVING FLAME PRESS, Locust Valley, N.Y. 11560

LIVING FLAME PRESS
BOX 74, LOCUST VALLEY, N.Y. 11560

Quantity

_____ Jonah — 1.75
_____ Poor in Spirit — 1.75
_____ And I Will Fill This House With Glory — 1.50
_____ Desert Silence — 1.75
_____ Praying With Scripture in the Holy Land — 2.25
_____ Discovering Pathways to Prayer — 1.75
_____ Reasons for Rejoicing — 1.75
_____ Contemplative Prayer — 1.75
_____ The One Who Listens — 2.25
_____ Enfolded by Christ — 1.95
_____ Petals of Prayer — 1.50
_____ Crisis of Faith — 1.50
_____ In God's Providence — 1.50
_____ Source of Life — 1.50
_____ Seeking Purity of Heart — 1.25
_____ Prompted by the Spirit — 2.25
_____ Discovering Pathways to Prayer — 1.75
_____ The Book of Revelation — 1.75
_____ Union With the Lord in Prayer — .85
_____ Attaining Spiritual Maturity — .85
_____ The Prayer of Love — 1.50
_____ Prayer, Aspiration and Contemplation — 3.95

QUANTITY ORDER: DISCOUNT RATES

For convents, prayer groups, etc.: $10 to $25 = 10%;
$26 to $50 = 15%; over $50 = 20%.
Booksellers: 40%, 30 days net.

NAME _____

ADDRESS _____

CITY_____ STATE_____ ZIP_____

☐ *Payment enclosed. Kindly include $.50 postage and handling on
order up to $5.00. Above that, include 10% of total up to $20.
Then 7% of total. Thank you.*